The

Decadent Cookbook

by Medlar Lucan and Durian Gray

Edited by Alex Martin and Jerome Fletcher

FOUR WALLS EIGHT WINDOWS, NEW YORK

Published in the United States by:
Four Walls Eight Windows
39 West 14th Street, # 503
New York, N.Y., 10011

Visit our website at http://www.4w8w.com

First U.S. printing September 2003.

First published by Dedalus, Ltd. Langford Lodge, St. Judith's Lane,
Sawdry, Cambs, PE 17 5XE, England.
Library of Congress Cataloging-in-Publication Data on file.
ISBN 1-56858-269-2

1 0   9   8   7   6   5   4   3   2   1

Printed in Canada

Designed and typeset by David Bird.
Front matter designed and typeset by Ink, Inc.

A SPECIAL NOTE FOR AMERICAN READERS OF

The Decadent Cookbook

Ah, America! The New Rome! As you stagger towards the apogee of Corruption and Grandeur we raise a glass of absinthe to you, hoping to summon up an apparition of the Green Fairy everywhere, from Hawaii to Cape Cod. And—while the purple dawn of Dissolution breaks like a peony from its sheath of night—we express the fond hope that American lovers of Decadence will rebuild the Decadent Restaurant amid the glittering ziggurats of Manhattan, Las Vegas or New Orleans. Take, Eat, Dream.

Medlar Lucan & Durian Gray

Contents

Introduction 9

1   Dinner with Caligula 13

2   The Grand Inquisitor's Breakfast 31

3   The Edible Galleon 51

4   The Gastronomic Mausoleum 67

5   Blood, the Vital Ingredient 83

6   Corruption and Decay 105

7   I Can Recommend the Poodle 115

8   The Decadent Sausage 139

9   The Marquis de Sade's Sweet Tooth 161

10   The Impossible Pudding 177

11   Angels and Devils 197

12   Postscript: Amblongus in Calabria 215

13   Conversion Table 221

ACKNOWLEDGMENTS

The editors would like to thank the following for their invaluable help:
Ciacio Arcangeli, Andrew and Ilia Bradbury, Professor J.B. Bullen, Roderick Conway Morris, Charles Baudelaire, Sara Ayad, Christine Donougher, Edward Gibbon, Susan Hitch, John and Lindsey Hoole, Joris-Karl Huysmans, Sören Jenson, Nicola Kennedy, Marina Malthouse, Sophie Martin, Anne Murcott, Anthony Neville, Charlotte Ward-Perkins, Tino Pugliese, Cassius Dio, Brian Stableford, Sara Sygare, Lotta Sygare, Vera at the Bodleian Library, and Jeff Young.

The editors would also like to thank the following for their permission to include the literary passage selected by Medlar Lucan and Durian Gray to be read aloud during dinner:

Louis de Bernières for *Labels* © Louis de Bernières 1993, David Madsen for an excerpt from *Memoirs of a Gnostic Dwarf* © David Madsen 1995, Brian Stableford for his translation of *A Glass of Blood* by Jean Lorrain taken from *The Dedalus Book of Decadence (Moral Ruins)* - edited by Brian Stableford and first published in 1990, Editions Gallimard in Paris for an excerpt from André Pieyre de Mandiargues *L'Anglais décrit dans le château fermé* © 1979 Editions Gallimard.

The editors would also like to thank Victor Gollancz Limited for permission to reproduce three recipes in The Decadent Sausage chapter from Antony & Araminta Hippisley Cox's *Book of Sausages* (1987).

The editors would also like to thank the Mansell Collection for permission to reproduce "The Ill-swept floor" a copy of a mosaic floor by Heralitus, A.D.200 and "My poor Medos, I shall be forced to eat you so that you can keep your poor master" an engraving by C. Hamlet after Drauer.

$\mathcal{J}$NTRODUCTION

For three brief but memorable years, Medlar Lucan and Durian Gray ran their own restaurant - The Decadent - on the first floor of a house in Edinburgh. It was a small, dark, luxurious place with a décor and atmosphere all its own. There were two dining-rooms: the first, as you walked in, panelled in ebony, the second hung with crimson and bottle-green silk. Deeper inside were three *cabinets particuliers*. These were snug little rooms, each about the size of a railway compartment, with a table that would seat up to six. *Cabinet N°1* was a monastic wooden box, bare, ascetic, penitential, with pale cream candles and pewter plates. *N°2* was the opposite - a sybarite's paradise upholstered in Fortuny silks and velvets, richly coloured, heavily perfumed. *N°3* was known as the Chart Room. It had a nautical theme (inspired by a passage in Huysmans' *A Rebours*) with portholes looking 'out' into tanks full of fish and lobsters, a ceiling hung with navigational equipment (sextants, dividers, compasses, etc.), coils of tarred rope, posters of transatlantic liners, and a speaking tube for sending out orders.

If you took one of these *cabinets* it was yours for the night - with no questions asked. Cushions, incense, musicians, liqueurs - any stimulants you cared to name - would be brought at any hour. The *cabinet*s made very wonderful couchettes. Sound did not travel between them, and they welcomed conspirators of every kind - artistic, political, amorous, or simply friends determined to shut out the world for a night.

The waiters were all young, male and very good-looking. Most were 'resting' actors. Their standard outfit was the long white apron, black trousers and bow tie of Renoir's café paintings, but you might equally see them as servants from Longhi's 18th century Venetian suppers, with powdered wigs, breeches and silk stockings; or costumed *à la turque* with *shalwar* and embroidered waistcoats. They could be Renaissance courtiers, Swiss guards, marshals of Napoleon's Grande Armée, hospital porters, airmen of the Second World War... Once, by special request, they blacked up, oiled their bodies, and wore nothing but white satin tangas.

They were often thought - wrongly - to be available for 'rent', and more than one lecherous alderman was presented with his bill earlier than he had bargained for after presuming too freely on this account.

A taste for the theatrical was also evident in the accoutrements of the place. Strange relics of gastronomic history would appear: food was served in a rare surviving example of Soyer's Magic Stove, birds were flamboyantly roasted on spits turned by a vastly complicated array of cogs, clockwork and chains; they had a replica of Rossini's famous silver syringe for injecting *pâté de foie gras* into macaroni; and the cutlery, napkins, pepper and salt came to the table in a *cadenas* - a boat-shaped vessel, made of gold, silver and enamelled copper, used by medieval French kings... These were the fruit of afternoons in antique-shops and auction-rooms, where Medlar's expert eye could pick out a single fine item from heaps of undistinguished junk.

Everything at The Decadent was idiosyncratic, but nothing more so than the food. Durian and Medlar poured all their turbulent energy, fantasy, playfulness and aesthetic extremism into a series of menus which managed simultaneously to make your mouth water and your hair stand on end. As well as being outrageous and unfailingly bizarre, the food was always exquisitely cooked. Even when you were eating cat in tomato sauce, stewed bull's genitalia, or armadillo sausages, you felt you were in safe hands.

Perhaps the most surprising thing about the food was its provenance. Very little - apart from odd details - came from the imagination. Almost everything was historical. Peasant cooking, *cuisine bourgeoise*, feasts for the rich and the royal - it was all equal to them, and they mixed it with a rare and delicate hand.

The guiding principles were simple: if anyone was likely to have tasted a dish before, they would not cook it; if it sounded shocking, improbable or just extravagant, they thought it worth a try. An odd colour, an unusual name, a quirky shape or historical connection was sometimes enough.

The wine list was also remarkable. As well as an excellent cellar they had an intriguing repertoire of cocktails that changed from week to week. One list went like this:

THUNDERCLAP

CINNAMON LIQUEUR

SNAKE IN THE GRASS

ABSINTHE

AURUM POTABILE

WHITE CURAÇOA (WYNAND FOCKINK 1961)

MILK PUNCH

KRUPNIK

They once made a working *pianocktail* - the instrument for mixing drinks described by Boris Vian in *L'Ecume des Jours*, which squirted a different alcohol into your glass for every note played. It was a complicated and magnificent structure, literally a 'piano-bar' with 88 different bottles suspended precariously above it - but the results were disastrous - or perhaps too successful. A customer drank a large *Saint Louis Blues* followed by a *Chattanooga Choo-Choo*, then danced the boogie-woogie with such reckless exuberance that he crashed into the nest of supply pipes that fed the pianocktail and destroyed its delicate mechanism.

The Decadent was, of course, too good to last. Despite a cult following, the business side never really held up, and Durian and Medlar were forced into ever more difficult choices between lowering their fastidious standards and raising their prices. The enmity of certain influential figures in the city didn't help. After three years of struggling to break even, The Decadent closed. Durian and Medlar vanished - some said to New York, others to Tasmania, others to the Far East.

Nothing was heard of them for over a year. Then one day a parcel arrived at the Dedalus office in Sawtry, wrapped in grey recycled paper and roughly tied with brown string. It was postmarked Calcutta. A brief covering letter from Medlar Lucan - written in his usual purple ink - offered the contents for publication: it was a collection of Decadent recipes together with

11

"notes and readings from our favourite authors". The text was clearly a joint effort, with chapters in somewhat different styles by the two of them - Medlar inclining to the theoretical, the literary and the morbid, while Durian indulged his taste for the festive, the spectacular, the grotesque. What follows is the contents of that parcel - The Decadent Cookbook - all that remains of a wicked and exciting place.

J.F.
A.M.

CHAPTER 1

DINNER WITH CALIGULA

He built tall sailing-ships of cedarwood, their poops and sterns set with precious stones, their sails of many colours, and within them baths, great galleries, promenades, and dining-chambers of vast capacity, containing vines and apple-trees and many other fruits; and here he would sit feasting all day among choirs of musicians and melodious singers, and so sail along the coasts of Campania.

This was Caius, also known as Caligula - one of a series of emperors who turned Rome in the 1st century AD from a city of strait-laced farmers and soldiers into a seething cosmopolis of aesthetes, gluttons and perverts. Thanks to the fabulous wealth of the empire, the patricians of Rome had little need to work. Taking their lead from the emperor, they indulged in lust, cruelty, violence and sensuality on a daily basis. Despite two thousand years of atrocities (politely known as 'history') that have passed since then, their excesses still send shivers along the spine.

The Decadents of 19th-century France loved the unashamed filth and self-indulgence of it all - the sadism of Tiberius, the insanity of Caligula, the joky viciousness of Nero. They could all have come straight from the pages of Huysmans or Gautier. Edward Gibbon, in his Decline and Fall of the Roman Empire, tells us that the emperor Heliogabalus 'abandoned himself to the grossest pleasures with ungoverned fury, and soon found disgust and satiety in the midst of his enjoyments... To confound the order of seasons and climates, to sport with the passions and prejudices of his subjects, and to subvert every law of nature and decency, were in the number of his most delicious amusements'. In other words, he was the perfect Decadent.

Eating was one of the great pleasures of the age. Murder was its great vice. Claudius was killed by a dish of his favourite mushrooms laced with poison. Heliogabalus was stabbed by his own guards, his body dragged through the streets and thrown into the River Tiber. Caligula, before being murdered himself, liked a good dose of death mixed with his meals. He watched his grandmother's funeral pyre burn from his dining-room, and had suspected criminals tortured and beheaded in front of him while he ate. His love of luxury was all-engulfing: he once gave dinner-guests an entire banquet made of gold, saying 'a man must either be frugal or else Caesar'.

While the poor of Rome ate porridge, bruised olives and sheep's lips, the rich feasted on the produce and spices of every known land - from Spain to China. Exotic foods, disguised foods, unlikely foods - these were all the rage. Sweet and sour sauces were an obsession. Heliogabalus ordered elephant trunk and roast camel from his kitchens, and spent a whole summer throwing parties where all the food was a single colour. The emperor Vitellius, who reigned from April to December 69 AD, was given a banquet by his brother where 2,000 of the most costly fish and 7,000 birds were served. His favourite dish, a monstrosity named 'The Shield of Minerva, Guardian of the City', included pheasants' and peacocks' brains, flamingoes' tongues, livers of wrasse and the roes of moray eels.

The only surviving Roman cookbook was written by Apicius, who liked nothing better than clashing flavours and the use of rare, improbable beasts. Dormice, flamingoes, sea-urchins, cranes - practically everything that moved was slaughtered and cooked and served up as wittily and elegantly as possible. 'They will not know what they are eating,' he boasted - 'anchovy stew without anchovies'! Apicius himself feasted his way through a huge fortune and then took poison rather than live a more modest life.

Dinner parties were a favourite entertainment. In fact they were the only entertainment (apart from sex in front of the slaves) available after dark. They began at the ninth hour (i.e. the ninth hour of daylight, between about 4 and 5 pm), usually after a work-out at the baths. They were long and sometimes very wild. There was music, dancing, flirting, petting, and of course sex. Suetonius says that Mark Antony 'took the wife of an ex-consul from her husband's dining-room, right before his eyes, and led her into a bedroom; he brought her back to the dinner party with her ears glowing and her hair dishevelled.' Caligula often did the same, adding a cynical commentary on the woman's performance when he came back to the table.

APICIAN NIGHTS

Roman banquets are fun to do, but however hard you try the food is unlikely to be completely authentic. (It may also turn out insipid or even disgusting - read the passage from Smollett's *Peregrine Pickle* as a warning). Apicius's cookbook, *De Re Coquinaria*, is still available, but the ancient methods of cooking and presenting food are lost for ever. Apicius gives no idea of quantities or cooking times, and there's even doubt about the identity of some ingredients.

Still, there's nothing to stop you having a go, so here's a simple checklist for a Do-It Yourself Dinner With Caligula:

◆ *Hire plenty of slaves for the evening*
◆ *Serve three courses: gustatio (hors d'oeuvres)*
                       fercula (entrées)
                       mensae secundae (dessert)
◆ *Lay on some entertainment (naughty friends, a good poet willing to read from his works, musicians, dancing girls from Cadiz)*
◆ *Provide guests with couches, finger bowls, vomit buckets, and large linen napkins*
◆ *Philosophy of the hour [declaimed by Trimalchio in Satyricon, as a slave dangled a silver skeleton before his guests]:*

> *'Look! Man is just a bag of bones.*
> *He's here, and gone tomorrow!*
> *We'll soon be like this fellow, so*
> *let's live! Let's drown our sorrow!'*

AN INVITATION

The poet Martial (c. 40-104 AD) issued dinner invitations to his friends in the form of verse 'Epigrams'. Perfectionists who know the difference between a hexameter and a place to park the car might like to try it too. This is one of Martial's best-known, *Cenabis bene*:

> *You shall eat well, Julius Cerialis, at my house;*
>
> *if you've nothing better to do, come round.*
>
> *Your eighth hour routine is safe: we can bathe together:*
>
> *you know the baths of Stephanus are just next door.*
>
> *First I shall give you lettuce, useful for stirring the bowels,*
>
> *and tender shoots of leek,*
>
> *pickled young tuna larger than a lizard,*
>
> *layered with eggs and leaves of rue;*
>
> *more eggs will follow, cooked gently on a low flame,*
>
> *with cheese from Velabrum Street*
>
> *and olives that have felt the Picenum frosts.*
>
> *That's the first course. Are you curious about the rest?*
>
> *I'll lie, to make sure you come: fish, oysters, sow's udders,*
>
> *stuffed fowl and marsh birds*
>
> *that not even Stella would serve at her rarest dinner.*
>
> *One more promise: I shall recite nothing,*
>
> *even if you read out your entire Gigantas*
>
> *or your pastorals, which are nearly as good as immortal Virgil's.*
>
> *(Epigrams, 11.52)*

Now it's time for some food.

We begin with the *gustatio* or

$\mathscr{H}$ORS $\mathscr{D}$'OEUVRES

The classic opener was eggs, which Martial smuggled in with tuna and rue, and then again (he obviously loved them) with cheese and olives. Apicius recommends serving them boiled with a garnish of pepper, lovage, nuts, honey, vinegar and fish-pickle.

A more decadent alternative is sea-urchins. These should be cooked in fish-stock, olive oil, sweet wine and pepper - and are best enjoyed, says Apicius, 'as one comes out of the bath.'

But enough of this coy stuff. Let's go for broke here, with one of the greatest of all Roman delicacies:

GLIRES
(ROAST DORMICE)

The dormouse, says Larousse, 'is a small rodent that nests in the branches of trees and feeds on nuts, berries, and seeds. In ancient times it was considered to be a delicacy.' The Romans bred them for the table in mud hutches and fed them on acorns through little holes. Unfortunately this is no longer done, so you must either find a very well-stocked butcher or take evening-classes in rodent-trapping. (Don't be tempted to use a hunting rifle, because the recipe calls for whole dormice.) If all else fails, you could go to a pet shop where they don't ask too many questions.

This is the recipe from Apicius:

Slit open and gut four dormice and stuff then with a mixture of minced pork and dormouse (all parts), pepper, nuts, stock, and laser (i.e. wild African fennel). Stitch up and roast on a tile or in a small clay oven.

Serve as they are, or as described in Satyricon, with honey and poppy-seeds.

If you can't get dormice, ask your butcher to do you a few ounces of minced pork or veal and some calf's brains; then, with squid from the fishmonger, you can cook this amphibian appetizer:

SIC FARCIES EAM SEPIAM COCTAM
(SQUID STUFFED WITH BRAINS)

Remove the membranes from a calf's brains, fry them and mash with pepper. Mix with raw eggs, peppercorns, and minced meat. Then stuff the mixture into the squid, stitch up and cook in boiling water until the stuffing is firm.

Still hungry? Then it's time for *fercula* or

*E*NTRÉES

LUMBULI
(SMALL ROAST TESTICLES)

Slice each testicle in two and sprinkle with pepper, nuts, finely chopped coriander and powdered fennel seed. Sew the halves together, wrap each one in a caul (i.e. the external membrane of a stomach) and fry them in olive oil and fish-pickle until brown. Then grill or roast in the oven.

IN STRUTHIONE ELIXO
(BOILED OSTRICH)

Boil an ostrich [easier if you do it in pieces] and set aside. In a pan make a sauce of pepper, mint, roast cumin, celery seed, dates, honey, vinegar, sweet wine, fish-stock and olive oil. Bring to the boil and thicken with starch. Lay out the boiled ostrich pieces on a dish and pour the sauce over them. Alternatively, boil the ostrich in the sauce, adding some spelt.

PORCELLUM HORTULANUM
(SUCKING PIG WITH VEGETABLES
AND GARDEN PESTS)

Have the pig boned from the neck down so that it resembles a bag. Make a stuffing of minced chicken, thrushes, fig-peckers, pork, Lucanian sausages, dates, bulbs, snails, mallows, beetroot, celery, leeks, cabbage, coriander, peppercorns, walnuts, 15 eggs and stock with pepper sauce. Truss, sear and roast in the oven. When cooked, split open the back and serve with a sauce of pepper, rue, stock, wine, honey, and oil, thickened with starch.

FLAMINGO STEW

Another dish for the intrepid. Flamingoes are not easy to find outside Africa, except in zoos. But guests will appreciate the effort, and you can do all sorts of exciting things with the plumage.

Pluck and gut a flamingo. Place in a pan with water, aniseed, salt and a little vinegar, and boil. When half cooked, add a bunch of chives and coriander leaves tied in a bundle. Towards the end of cooking, add some boiled wine to give it colour.

Take a pestle and mortar and grind up pepper, cumin, coriander, laser root, mint and rue. Add vinegar, dates and some of the cooking broth, then pour the lot into the pan. Thicken the sauce with starch, then serve.

You can use the same recipe for parrot.

Sauce for roast flamingo

Grind pepper, lovage, celery seed, parsley, mint, dried onion, fried sesame seeds and dates with a pestle and mortar. Pour in wine, honey, stock, olive oil, vinegar and boiled wine. Mix well.

Turdos

(stewed thrushes)

A less spectacular dish, showing that the Romans could use everyday ingredients in interesting ways. The Latin name also makes a certain splash.

Make a stuffing for the thrushes as follows: grind pepper, laser and laurel berries, then add cumin and fish-pickle. Insert this through the bird's throat then stitch up the hole. Stew the thrushes in oil and water seasoned with salt, aniseed and leeks.

Haedus sive agnus syringatus id est mammotestis

(kid or lamb hollowed out like a pipe)

The preparation of this dish calls for a strong stomach and a powerful pair of lungs. As few Decadents will be equipped with either of these, they may prefer to have the 'emptying' as well as the 'bagging' done by a butcher.

Have the animal boned from the neck down so that it resembles a bag. Empty the intestines by blowing into the head, forcing the contents out of the lower end; then wash them very carefully with water. Stuff the intestines with a mixture of your choosing. Sew up the body at the shoulder and roast in the oven, or boil in a basket lowered into a cauldron of salted water. Serve in a sauce made of milk, pepper, stock, wine and olive oil, thickened with starch.

Mensae Secundae

(DESSERTS)

PATINAM DE ROSIS
(ROSE-HIP AND CALF'S BRAIN CUSTARD)

Pound some rose hips with a little stock in a mortar. Add $^1/8$ pint stock, strain through a colander, then set aside. Take 4 calves' brains (membranes removed), then grind them up with 8 scruples ($^1/3$ oz.) of pepper. Mix with the rose hip stock. Break 8 eggs, and mix them with $^1/8$ pint wine, $^1/12$ pint raisin wine and a little olive oil. Combine this with the brains and stock, pour into a greased dish and cook on hot ashes. Serve with finely ground black pepper.

COCHLEAS LACTE PASTAS
(MILK-FED SNAILS)

Gather some snails, wipe them clean, and remove the membrane that seals the opening of their shells. Put them in a bowl of milk with a little salt for a day, then for a few days in plain milk. Dredge out their droppings every hour. When the snails are too fat to get back into their shells, fry them in olive oil. Serve with wine sauce.

OVA SPONGIA EX LACTE
(OMELETTE WITH HONEY)

Beat four eggs with half a pint of milk. Heat some olive oil in a pan, add the eggs and milk and cook until they form a sponge. Serve on a round dish with honey and pepper.

INE

No Roman banquet would be complete without wine - although you may prefer not to be too authentic about this as the Romans drank their wine very sweet - 3 parts golden syrup to 4 parts Liebfraumilch will give you an idea. Sweetening was the usual method of preserving wine from the attentions of vinegar bacteria (another was mixing it with sea-water, which must have been extremely unpleasant). Wine was often flavoured with herbs and watered down before drinking. It probably tasted like sweet Martini or Cinzano.

As to the Roman manner of drinking wine, here's Juvenal in his Sixth Satire:

She arrives from the baths, red-faced; she is so thirsty that she would drink the entire contents of a wine-urn placed at her feet. Before she eats, she takes a second sextarius - this will give her a frenzied appetite once she has thrown up on the floor and her stomach is well washed. Streams run along the marble; the golden bowl exhales the aroma of Falernian wine. Like a long snake that has fallen to the bottom of a barrel she drinks and vomits.

Roman men, of course, were far less delicate in their drinking habits.

Here are two recipes for flavoured wines from Apicius:

CONDITUM PARADOXUM
(WINE STRANGELY SPICED)

Pour 2 pints of wine and 15 lb of honey into a bronze pot. The wine will be boiled off as the honey melts. Heat on a slow fire, using dry wood, and stir with a wooden stick. Pour in more wine if it starts to boil over. Remove the fire and let the contents of the pot settle and grow cold. Then light another fire under the pot, boil it up again, let it cool. Repeat a third time. After this you can move the pot off the hearth. Next day, skim the wine, add 4 oz of ground pepper, 3 scruples (half a teaspoon) of mastic, a handful of saffron, the same of spikenard (or bay) leaves, and five dried dates soaked in wine until soft. Then pour in 18 pints of mild wine, mix, and serve hot or cold.

ROSATUM ET VIOLACIUM
(ROSE OR VIOLET WINE)

Take a large quantity of rose or violet petals, sew them into a linen bag, and soak them in wine for seven days. Then remove the petals and replace them with fresh ones. Leave these in the wine for another seven days. Repeat a third time. Then filter the wine and mix with honey before serving. Take care to use only the best and freshest petals, gathered after the dew has dried.

A Carthaginian Feast

By Gustave Flaubert

Men of all nations were there, Ligurians and Lusitanians, Balearic Islanders, Negroes, and fugitives from Rome . . .

They lay upon cushions; they squatted around huge trays, and so ate; others, lying upon their bellies, reached out for lumps of meat and gorged themselves, leaning on their elbows in the placid posture of lions dismembering their prey. Late-comers, leaning against the trees, watched the low tables half hidden under the scarlet coverings, and awaited their turn.

Since Hamilcar's kitchens were inadequate, the Council had provided slaves, dishes and couches. Oxen were roasting at great clear fires in the middle of the garden, which thus looked like a battlefield when the dead are being burned. Loaves dusted with aniseed vied with huge cheeses heavier than disks, and great bowls of wine with mighty water tankards, set close to gold filigree baskets full of flowers. Their eyes gleamed wide in delight at being at last free to gorge to their hearts' content; and here and there they were beginning to sing.

First they were served with birds in green sauce upon plates of red clay, decorated in black relief; then with every kind of shell-fish that is found on the Punic coasts, with broths thickened with wheat, beans and barley, and with cumin-spiced snails upon yellow amber dishes.

After this the tables were loaded with meats: antelopes still with their horns, peacocks still with their feathers, whole sheep cooked in sweet wine, camels' and buffaloes' haunches, hedgehogs in garum sauce, fried grasshoppers, and pickled dormice. Great pieces of fat were floating amid saffron in bowls of Tamrapanni wood. Everywhere was a lavish abundance of pickles, truffles, and asafoetida. There were pyramids of fruit tumbling upon honeycombs; and they had not forgotten to serve some of those silky-coated, red, fat-paunched little dogs, fattened on olive lees: a Carthaginian dish which was an abomination to other peoples. Their stomachs' greed was titillated by the excitement and wonder of such novel fare. The Gauls, with their long hair coiled upon the top of their heads, snatched at water-melons and lemons, and crunched them peel and all. Negroes who had never seen a crawfish, tore their faces on its red spines. The Greeks, who were smooth-shaven and whiter than marble, threw the leavings of their plates behind them; while herdsmen from Brutium, clad in wolf-skins, ate in silence, their faces buried in their plates.

Night fell. The awning over the cypress avenue was drawn back, and torches were brought.

G. Flaubert, *Salammbo* (transl. by Powys Mathers).

A ROMAN BANQUET

by T. G. Smollett

The doctor . . . with an air of infinite satisfaction, . . . began: - "This here, gentlemen, is a boiled goose, served up in a sauce composed of pepper, lovage, coriander, mint, rue, anchovies, and oil! I wish for your sakes, gentlemen, it was one of the geese of Ferrara, so much celebrated among the ancients for the magnitude of their livers, one of which is said to have weighed upwards of two pounds; with this food, exquisite as it was, did the tyrant Heliogabalus regale his hounds. But I beg pardon. I had almost forgot the soup, which I hear is so necessary an article at all tables in France. At each end there are dishes of the falacacabia of the Romans; one is made of parsley, penny-royal, cheese, pine-tops, honey, vinegar, brine, eggs, cucumbers, onions, and hen-livers; the other is much the same as the *soup-maigre* of this country. Then there is a loin of veal boiled with fennel and caraway seed, on a pottage composed of pickle, oil, honey and flour, and a curious *hachis* of the lights, liver and blood of an hare, together with a dish of roasted pigeons. Monsieur le Baron shall I help you to a plate of this soup?" The German, who did not all approve of the ingredients, assented to the proposal, and seemed to relish the composition; while the marquis . . . was in consequence of his desire accommodated with a portion of the *soup-maigre*; and the count . . . supplied himself with a pigeon . . .

The Frenchman, having swallowed the first spoonful, made a pause; his throat swelled as if an egg had stuck in his gullet, his eyes rolled, and his mouth underwent a series of involuntary contractions and dilations. Pallet, who looked steadfastly at this connoisseur, with a view of consulting his taste, before he himself would venture upon the soup, began to be disturbed at these emotions, and observed with some concern, that the poor gentleman seemed to be going into a fit; when Peregrine assured him that these were symptoms of ecstasy, and for further confirmation, asked the marquis how he found the soup. It was with infinite difficulty that his complaisance could so far master his disgust, as to enable him to answer, "Altogether excellent, upon my honour!" And the painter, being certified of his approbation, lifted the spoon to his mouth without scruple; but far from justifying the eulogium of his taster, when this precious composition diffused itself upon his palate, he seemed to be deprived of all sense and motion, and sat like the leaded statue of some river god, with the liquor flowing out at both sides of his mouth.

The doctor, alarmed at this indecent phenomenon, earnestly inquired into the cause of it; and when Pallet recovered his recollection, and swore that he would rather swallow porridge made of burning brimstone, than such an infernal mess as that which he had tasted; the physician, in his own vindication, assured the company, that, except the usual ingredients, he had mixed nothing in the soup but some sal-armoniac instead of the ancient nitrum, which could not now be procured; and appealed to the marquis, whether such a succedaneum was not an improvement of the whole. The unfortunate *petit-maître*, driven to the extremity of his condescension, acknowledged it to be a masterly refinement; and deeming himself obliged, in point of honour, to evince his sentiments by his practice, forced a few more mouthfuls of this disagreeable potion down his throat, till his stomach was so much offended that he was compelled to start up of a sudden; and, in the hurry of his elevation, overturned his plate into the bosom of the baron. The emergency of his occasions would not permit him to stay and make apologies for this abrupt behaviour; so that he flew into another apartment, where Pickle found him puking, and crossing himself with great devotion; and a chair, at his desire, being brought to the door, he slipped into it, more dead than alive

... When our hero returned to the dining-room ... the places were filled with two pies, one of dormice liquored with syrup of white poppies which the doctor had substituted in the room of toasted poppy-seed, formerly eaten with honey, as a dessert; and the other composed of a hock of pork baked in honey.

Pallet hearing the first of these dishes described, lifting up his hands and eyes, and with signs of loathing and amazement pronounced, "A pye made of dormice and syrup of poppies; Lord in heaven! what beastly fellows those Romans were!" ... All the doctor's invitations and assurances could not prevail upon his guest to honour the *hachis* and the goose; and that course was succeeded by another ... "That which smoaks in the middle," said he, "is a sow's stomach, filled with a composition of minced pork, hogs brains, eggs, pepper, cloves, garlick, aniseed, rue, oil, wine, and pickle. On the right-hand side are the teats and belly of a sow, just farrowed, fried with sweet wine, oil, flour, lovage, and pepper. On the left is a fricassee of snails, fed, or rather purged, with milk. At that end next Mr. Pallet are fritters of pompions, lovage, origanum, and oil; and here are a couple of pullets, roasted and stuffed in the manner of Apicius."

The painter, who had by wry faces testified his abhorrence of the sow's stomach, which he compared to a bagpipe, and the snails which had undergone purgation, no sooner heard him mention the roasted pullets, than he eagerly solicited the wing of a fowl; ... but scarce were they set down before him, when the tears ran down his cheeks, and he called aloud in a manifest disorder, "Z———ds! this is the essence of a whole bed of garlic!" That he might not, however, disappoint or disgrace the entertainer, he applied his instruments to one of the birds; and when he opened up the cavity, was assaulted by such an irruption of intolerable smells, that, without staying to disengage himself from the cloth, he sprung away, with an exclamation of "Lord Jesus!" and involved the whole table in havoc, ruin, and confusion.

Before Pickle could accomplish his escape, he was sauced with the syrup of the dormouse-pye, which went to pieces in the general wreck; and as for the Italian count, he was overwhelmed by the sow's stomach, which bursting in the fall, discharged its contents upon his leg and thigh, and scalded him so miserably, that he shrieked with anguish, and grinned with a most ghastly and horrible aspect. . .

The doctor was confounded with shame and vexation . . . he expressed his sorrow for the misadventure . . . and protested there was nothing in the fowls which could give offence to a sensible nose, the stuffing being a mixture of pepper, lovage, and assafoetida, and the sauce consisting of wine and herring-pickle, which he had used instead of the celebrated garum of the Romans.

T. G. Smollett, *Peregrine Pickle.*

Chapter 2

The Grand
Inquisitor's Breakfast

We stay in Rome - city of eternal Decadence - to visit the kitchens of a much craftier set of princes: the Renaissance popes. These were men who had read Machiavelli, absorbed his lessons, and instead of being knifed and chucked into the Tiber at the age of 30 were allowed to die of old age, given magnificent funerals, and then canonized.

One of these was Antonio Ghislieri (better known as Pius V), remembered now as an 'ascetic, reformer, and relentless persecutor of heretics, whose papacy marked one of the most austere periods in Roman Catholic Church history.' He was born into a poor family in 1504, worked as a shepherd, became a monk, then joined the Inquisition. He was so keen on his job of rooting out error that he worried even the man who had appointed him, Pius IV. He became Grand Inquisitor in 1558, and Pope in 1566. On his election he introduced immediate reforms to church practices, and harsh new punishments for Sunday desecration, animal baiting and other profane activities. A decree published in Rome on 2 October 1566 says, "To prevent many evil customs and vices, both of the mouth and of gaming, lust, blasphemy, thieving and other unspeakable crimes, which are born from the abuse of inns and taverns, to the dishonour of our Lord God, to the harm of the inhabitants of this Holy City and the scandal of other peoples and nations... all persons residing in Rome or Borghi, and all prostitutes and dishonest women are forbidden to frequent inns and taverns in Rome and Borghi, to eat, drink, play cards, dice or other games, or do other illicit and dishonest things either openly or in secret. The penalty will be 25 golden scudi and three lashes; prostitutes and dishonest women will be whipped and imprisoned, with further punishments according to our judgement... Anyone informing on innkeepers or other prohibited persons guilty of infringement of this ban will be rewarded with one scudo per person accused."

The good times were definitely over. But not just for gamblers, innkeepers and prostitutes: priests had to spend more time in their parishes, and monks and nuns who took vows of seclusion were forced to stop going to parties and actually shut themselves away from the world. Nepotism was outlawed, corrupt monastic orders suppressed, and dissident intellectuals driven into exile or burnt at the stake. In March 1571, Pius published a list of books which he regarded as morally degrading or un-Christian, and hundreds of printers fled to Switzerland and Germany. He forced Jews to live in ghettos, and encouraged tyranny, ruthlessness and intolerance in Catholic rulers, threatening them with the wrath of God if they spared the lives of heretics. "Let them perish," he wrote, "in the agony they deserve." He died regretting only one thing: that he had been too lenient.

How did this merciless patron of prosecutors eat? Was he a dry bread and water man, or did he sit down after a hard day at the Inquisition and wallow in papal troughs of gluttony?

His portrait on a medallion shows a cunning, weaselish face, hollow-cheeked and sharp-nosed, buried in thought. It's impossible to guess what's on his mind. But a cookbook published in 1570 by his chef, Bartolomeo Scappi, suggests that Pius was no stranger to the pleasures of the table. Among many fine dishes proposed by Scappi are fried birds' tongues (first tasted at Cardinal Grimano's in Venice), pig's blood omelette, stuffed squid, boneless frog soup, barbecued bear, spitted calf's head, baked dormice, roast hedgehog, and a range of interesting pies: snail pie, tortoise-innard pie, frog's liver pie, and a puff-pastry *crostata* made with the sweetbreads, eyes, ears and testicles of a young goat. We could still be in ancient Rome.

Scappi has lots of useful ideas for Decadent cooks: his black broth makes an excellent starter, with its lush blend of quinces, raisins, prunes, black cherries, grape juice, red wine, pepper, cinnamon, nutmeg, cloves, crushed fruit-cakes, Seville orange juice, and sugar. Menus are given for every month of the year, including Lent and fast-days, and what to serve if the Emperor Charles V comes to lunch (he expected at least 400 dishes). There's also a handy appendix: *Il Trinciante* (the Carver) by Vincenzo Cervio, which tells you how to cut up everything, including peacocks, cranes, oysters, wild pig's heads, crabs, thrushes, melons and eggs.

Scappi knew how to furnish a table, and the Decadent faced

with entertaining a party of dandies, bishops or chief constables for breakfast could do worse than use this menu - originally served after Vespers in a garden in Trastevere on a May morning.

The table was laid with three table-cloths and decorated with a variety of flowers and leafy boughs, the wines were various, both sweet and dry, the sideboard furnished with cups of gold, silver, majolica and glass. A large bun made with milk, eggs, sugar and butter was placed under each napkin, and scented water was offered for the guests' hands. There were eight stewards and four carvers. Fresh white napkins were given with every change of the table-cloth. Gold and silver knives and forks were used for the savouries and spoons for the sweets. Each course was accompanied by six statues: the first made of sugar, the second of butter, the third of sweet almond pastry. Music, played on a variety of instruments, accompanied the meal.

$\mathcal{F}$IRST $\mathcal{C}$OURSE

WITH SUGAR STATUES

DIANA WITH THE MOON, BOW AND ARROWS,

DOGS ON A LEASH, AND FIVE NYMPHS.

FIRST NYMPH HOLDING A SPEAR.

SECOND NYMPH WITH A BOW AND QUIVER.

THIRD WITH A VIOLA.

FOURTH WITH A BUGLE.

FIFTH WITH A CYMBAL.

8 plates of each of the following:

Preserved yellow cherries, strawberries with sugar, candied grapes, sweet oranges with sugar, Neapolitan fruit cakes, marzipan lozenges, miniature almond pastries, sweet pine-seed cakes, buns, cream cheeses with sugar, syringed butter sprinkled with sugar, junkets served in leaves with sugar and flowers, sliced fish-roes with lemon juice and sugar, pickled sturgeon and herrings, tuna fish charcuterie, pickled anchovies, asparagus salad, sugared caper and raisin salad, salad of sliced citrons with sugar and rose-water, lettuce and borage flower salad, cold trout pies, butter tartlets, Spanish olives, mushrooms stuffed with rice à la turque.

The first table-cloth was removed and perfumed water offered for the guests' hands.

$\mathscr{S}$ECOND $\mathscr{C}$OURSE

WITH SIX BUTTER STATUES

AN ELEPHANT WITH A CASTLE ON ITS BACK,

HERCULES STRANGLING THE LION,

A LARGE CAMPIDOGLIO RUSTIC,

A CAMEL RIDDEN BY A MOORISH KING,

A UNICORN WITH ITS HORN IN A SERPENT'S MOUTH,

MELEAGER'S BOAR WITH AN ARROW IN ITS BREAST.

8 plates of each of the following:

Tender peas boiled in their pods with vinegar and pepper dressing; cooked artichoke hearts in vinegar, salt and pepper; truffles cooked in oil, Seville orange juice and pepper; artichokes fried in butter served with Seville orange juice and pepper; raw truffles served with salt and pepper; small Neapolitan palms; pear tarts; pears in wine and sugar; fresh musk-pears; yellow morello cherries; Florentine raviggiolo cheeses; sliced Parmesan cheese; March cheeses served in halves; fresh almonds on vine leaves; preserved grapes; cream cheeses with sugar; wafer rolls; small circular buns; roast chestnuts stewed in rose-water and served with sugar, salt and pepper; turnip compôte, carrot compôte, cucumber compôte, samphire compôte.

The table-cloth was removed and water offered for the guests' hands. Change of spoons, forks and napkins.

WITH ALMOND PASTRY STATUES

PARIS HOLDING A GOLDEN APPLE,

PALLAS ATHENE NUDE,

JUNO NUDE,

VENUS NUDE,

GOLDEN-HAIRED HELEN OF TROY CLOTHED,

EUROPA ON A BULL WITH HER HANDS ON THE HORNS.

8 cups of each of the following preserved fruit :

Citrons, small lemons, small bitter oranges, water-melons, melons, pumpkins, pears, peaches, apricots; pickled nutmegs and walnuts.

8 plates of each of the following:

Wild cherries in syrup, quince jelly in boxes, quince marmalade in boxes, Sienese nougat in boxes, quince cakes, boxes of sugared aniseed, boxes of large sweets, sugared melon seeds, sugared coriander seeds, sugared almonds, pistachios, fennel and pine-seeds.

40 bunches of flowers, their stems wrapped in silk and gold.
40 toothpicks scented with rose-water.

All this is fine for Sunday breakfast, of course, but what about more everyday fare - the midweek supper, the working lunch? Here are a few more dishes from the Grand Inquisitor's table.

FROGS

THEIR SIZE AND SEASON

———•·•·•———

Frogs are small tail-less animals, green and yellow in colour, with white bellies. They live in fresh water and swamps, and have a variety of cries. They are very plentiful in Italy, especially in Lombardy and around Bologna, where you can see them carried along in sackloads on carts.

This little animal has a large liver from which pies can be made. Its season runs from May until the end of October. This is also the time of verjuice (green grapes), so while grapes are green frogs are in season.

TO FRY AND SERVE FROGS IN VERJUICE

(JUICE OF SOUR GRAPES)

———•·•·•———

Cut off the frog's head, which has a large mouth, and the ends of its legs up to the first joint. Soak in fresh water for 8 hours, changing the water from time to time. This purges and deflates them and blanches the meat. Take them out of the water. To fry, fold the legs under, or cut off the thighs and remove the thigh-bones, then dip them in flour and fry them in oil. Serve hot with a little pounded salt on top.

Once they are fried they must never be covered or kept for very long as they become tough and lose their goodness. They can also be fried with cloves of boiled garlic and parsley. Serve with garlic, parsley, pepper, and pounded salt, which is how Pope Pius IV of happy memory used to eat them in 1564, served by me.

After frying simply in flour they can also be conserved in

fresh verjuice and egg yolks, and served hot or cold as you like. Or they can be fried and served with fennel leaves, basil, garlic cloves, breadcrumbs soaked in verjuice, salt and pepper. Or cover with garlic sauce and hazelnuts in the Milanese style.

BONELESS FROG SOUP

Soak the frogs as above, then put them in plain water; bring to the boil, remove from the hot water, put them in cold water, remove the meat from the thighs and put it in a pan with butter or oil and fry gently with a little crushed onion, adding some of the white water they were cooked in, & gooseberries or sour grapes, sweet spices, a touch of saffron, and at the end a few crushed fresh herbs; serve hot. If you don't want to use onions, add crushed almonds or breadcrumbs to thicken the broth.

You can also cook this soup in the same way leaving the bones in.

BEAR

COOKED IN VARIOUS WAYS

Bear has to be caught young and in the right season, which is winter. In July the bear is fatter as a result of feeding, but its meat gives off a bad smell.

First skin the bear. Take the best parts - its thighs - and leave them to hang for a few days. To roast them on the spit, first grill them for a while unlarded, then sprinkle with salt, fennel, pepper, cinnamon, and cloves, and cook as you would a goat, i.e. on a slow fire, collecting the fat that drips off. Serve hot with a sauce made of rosé vinegar, sugar, salt, fennel, pepper, cinnamon, and cloves, and the reserved fat from the cooking.

You can make the same dishes from bear that you make from stag. The heads of bears are not good to eat, and are usually avoided. The meat is not much eaten either, although I have on occasion cooked it.

PORCUPINE

COOKED IN VARIOUS WAYS

———•◦•———

Catch the porcupine at its fattest in the month of August, but avoid it from October to January, when its meat has a miserable smell. Let the meat hang for four days in winter, one and a half days in summer. Remove the skin and cut the body in half, crosswise. Lard the rear half by studding it with pieces of fat rolled in pepper, cinnamon, cloves, nutmeg and salt. The pieces should be quite big and cover the meat completely. Add some garlic, cloves and rosemary to take away the bad smell, then roast the meat on a spit, collecting the juices. Serve hot with a sauce made of cooked grape-must, rosé vinegar, pepper, cinnamon, cloves and the roasting juices.

Alternatively you can spit-roast porcupine whole, or stuff it as you would a baby goat* and roast in the oven. The fore-parts can also be used to make a rich, fatty broth by adapting the recipe for goat.**

Another method is to cut the meat in pieces and boil it, then fry in lard with chopped onions and serve with a sauce of strained green grape-juice, pepper and cinnamon. The innards, apart from the liver, are inedible. You can prepare fresh porcupine livers as you would goat's - remove the membrane and fry in lard or roast on a spit, either whole or in pieces (if spit-roasting pieces, stuff them in a caul first).

* BABY GOAT: make the stuffing with fat, chopped ham, liver and other offal, prunes and dried morello cherries (or, in summer, gooseberries, green grapes or any underripe fruit), unsalted cheese, and eggs.

** GOAT: wash the meat with wine and water, strain the washing liquid into an earthenware or copper pot. Add the meat, then pepper, cinnamon, nutmeg, fat, diced ham, a few leaves of sage, some raisins, cooked must or sugar, prunes and dried morello cherries. Cook on a low heat with the pot tightly lidded for one and a half hours, and serve hot. You can also add ground almonds or whole onions which have been previously half-cooked in embers.

GUINEA-PIGS AND DORMICE

Some people call the *coniglio d'India* [literally, India-rabbit] a 'piglet', because it has a pointed snout, small round ears, a light skin and hairs which are more reminiscent of a pig's bristles than wool. To roast a guinea-pig on the spit, remove the hairs with hot water, take out its innards, and stuff it as you would a baby goat - using a mixture of fat, pounded ham, offal (which should be well washed), spices, prunes and dried sour cherries, fat unsalted cheese and eggs. In summer you can use gooseberries, verjuice or musk pears, or any under-ripe fruit instead of the prunes and cherries. Finally, spit and roast on a slow fire.

Guinea-pigs can also be roasted without a stuffing, on a spit or in the oven.

This method also suits dormice, which are small animals with long, hairy tails, pointed faces and very sharp teeth. They live in chestnut and walnut trees, eating the fruit. Their season is from October to the end of February, which is when they are fattest. This is the same season as the guinea-pig, although in Rome and other parts of Italy you can find both animals all year round.

PEACOCK

The peacock is well known for its beautiful feathers. It has a purple neck, a small crest on its head, a long tail marked with purple eyes, and large black feet. Some peacocks are white. Peacock meat is black but tastier than that of any other bird.

To roast a peacock on a spit, take an old bird in season (October to the end of February) and hang it after death for eight days without plucking or removing its innards. It is best to pluck peacocks dry rather than using water, which spoils the taste and breaks the skin. After plucking the bird, take out the innards, leaving the neck and the feet with their feathers on. Cut off the wings, clean the blood from the inside of the body with a white linen cloth, then pass a hot iron poker through the hole where the innards were extracted, taking care not to touch the meat: this dries up the moisture and takes away any foul odours.

To stuff the bird, use the general stuffing recipe*, or sprinkle with salt, fennel leaves, pepper, cloves, cinnamon, and stuff the body with dried fennel seeds, a piece of good fresh fat studded with cloves or fine pieces of saveloy partly cooked in water or over coals, and stud the breast with cloves. Cook on a slow fire, and keep the neck with its feathers on. Serve hot or cold with a variety of sauces.

* GENERAL STUFFING RECIPES FOR ALL SPIT-ROASTED ANIMALS: take four pounds of fat (which should not be rancid), and shred it finely with knives. Add 2 lb of chopped kid's or other liver, mint, marjoram, parsley and salad burnet, four raw egg-yolks, half an ounce each of pepper and cinnamon, a quarter ounce each of ground nutmeg and cloves, half a pound of mixed prunes and dried morello cherries, (or in summer gooseberries or green grapes). Mix them all well together. You can choose whether or not to add grated cheese, garlic and fried scallions.

You can do this in another way: mix 4 lb of shredded fat with the same amount of lean veal, mutton or pork, without skin or nerves. Add four and a half ounces of ham, spices as above, 4 ounces of raisins, and a few boiled artichoke stems, good mushrooms or truffles.

Another way is to mix the fat with 2 lb of boiled calf or kid sweetbreads, 1 lb of yellow saveloy mixture, 4 ounces of sugar, four egg-yolks, a handful of herbs, new plums that are not too ripe, black figs or musk-pears without the flower, not forgetting spices as above. Instead of sweetbreads you can use boiled calf's, pig's or kid's brains.

Another way is mix the fat with 2 lb of boiled and grated liver from one of these animals, with one ounce of dried sweet fennel either crumbled or crushed, 6 egg yolks, 4 ounces of sugar, a handful of finely chopped herbs, 1 lb of grated cheese, one and a half ounces of the spices mentioned above, and some boiled cloves of good garlic.

'LIVE' PEACOCK WITH SMALL BIRDS

Skin the peacock, starting from the breast, leaving the head, wings, tail and feet attached to the skin. When it's gutted and cooked, let it cool and arrange a piece of iron in the shape of a half moon to grip the middle of the body, and another piece in the shape of the moon to go through the neck; another half-moon piece lower than the first to hold up the tail, and two small rods inserted into the thighs. Then carefully stretch the skin over the body, arranging it so that the neck, tail and feet stand firm on the irons, and the whole thing looks as if it is alive. You can fill the body with a variety of small live birds, and put fire in its mouth using acqua vitae and camphor or other substances. The board should be surrounded with branches of boxwood or myrtle, and there should be a hole under the wings so that when the Carver begins to carve the birds can fly out.

MEMOIRS OF A GNOSTIC DWARF

by David Madsen

During the carnival week last year, Leo and I attended a most extraordinary banquet given by Lorenzo Strozzi, the banker, brother of Filippo Strozzi, who is well known in Rome (and perhaps beyond) for his epicurean inclinations; Leo came dressed as a cardinal, wearing a silly sort of eye-mask of black velvet. Nobody was supposed to know he was there, apparently, but as Cardinals Rossi, Cibo, Salviati and Ridolfi were also present, this absurd attempt at incognito was somewhat futile.

We were all led up a flight of steps to a door which had been painted black, through which we entered a large hall, entirely draped in black silk and velvet; in the middle of this hall stood a black table on which reposed two black glass flagons of wine and two human skulls, filled with the very choicest viands.

"Do you think the poor man is depressed?" Leo whispered to me.

"No. We're meant to be mystified, or a little frightened, or perhaps both."

After nibbling for a while, everyone was ushered into an adjoining hall, even larger, which was blindingly, brilliantly lit by innumerable candles and oil-lamps, some of the most exquisite execution, in gold and silver, adorned with precious stones. I caught Leo eyeing them enviously. We sat down at the huge table, and after some moments were surprised - not to say shocked - by a deep rumbling beneath our chairs; one or two of the ladies swooned, and Cardinal Ridolfi, ridiculous old actress that he is, leapt to his feet with a squeal of horror and announced:

"The apocalypse has begun!"

In fact, it was the sound of a mechanical contrivance beneath the floor, which was so designed (cleverly, I concede, but all rather *de trop*) as to allow a great circular board to rise up from the room below, through the floor, until it was precisely level with the table at which we sat, and on it was heaped great dishes of victuals. Relieved more than anything else, several of the guests burst into applause. Lorenzo Strozzi allowed himself the faint trace of a smile, like a magician gratified at the success of his first trick, but knowing that there are even better ones to come. As indeed there were.

Servants placed a chased silver platter in front of each guest, who found, to his or her consternation, that what it contained was quite inedible. There were little cries of horror or delight or bewilderment; there was oddly forced laughter; some people began to look more than a little frightened.

"What have you got in yours?" I asked Leo.

He peered down at his plate and sniffed.

"It would appear to be half a pair of female undergarments," he answered. "Boiled."

"I've got a raw sausage."

"An empty eggshell!" a voice cried.

"A toad - oh Jesus - a *live* toad!" shrieked another, less enthusiastically.

"The heel of a shoe -"

"A kerchief, fried in batter. . ."

"Good God Almighty - a penis! No, no, wait a moment - ah! A blanched baby marrow, I think -"

Suddenly, the lights were extinguished. Quite how Strozzi managed it, I do not know; maybe there were servants hidden behind the drapes - in fact, now I come to think of it, this is the only way it *could* have been done. The great hall immediately rang with the shrill screams and shrieks of all the ladies, and Cardinal Ridolfi. Then we heard the slow rumble and shudder of the mechanism again, which was clearly being lowered, freshly loaded, and sent up a second time. After this, the candles were re-lighted (which took some time), and - behold! - the great table at which we sat was laden. This time the applause was strenuous and prolonged.

For the first course we were served vegetable soup with *stracciatelli*, and *potage à la royne*, which were accompanied by enormous slices of bread fried in oil and garlic and piled high with finely minced and seasoned partridge and pheasant, decorated with *funghi porcini*, artichokes deep-fried in the Jewish manner (Strozzi was a banker, after all), and baby onions. There was also a *potage garni* accompanied by all manner of offal (which I heartily dislike, but in any case my Gnostic principles would not permit me to eat any of the meat.)

The second course consisted of venison broiled in stock, pies of every variety, pressed tongue, spiced sausages and salamis served with chopped melon and figs, and savoury egg flans. These delicacies were followed by huge roasts: more partridges and pheasants, larks (their tongues, basted in honey and orange with *basilico*, served separately), wood doves, pigeons, young chickens, and whole lambs. Then came a huge array of dishes made from butter, eggs and cheese - pies, flans, pastries, and so on; bowls of *melanzane* marinated in white wine and sprinkled lavishly with fragrant herbs, celery chopped with onions and peppers drenched in oil, also put in an appearance. The wines flowed as freely as a drunkard's piss.

After several hours of continuous eating, I was feeling quite faint; indeed, I could not imagine how so many of the other guests were still happily cramming themselves. Leo, unsurprisingly, chomped his way through the lot; however, he had not as yet farted (although I expected a real stinker at any moment), which was some small blessing. Lorenzo Strozzi, at the head of the table, finally rose to his feet a little unsteadily.

"Your Holiness - ah - Your Eminences, I meant to say, of course! - my dear and very *special* guests! I offer you now the climax, the apotheosis, the summit of this rather *unusual* evening."

He clapped his hands, and four servants entered the hall, bearing on their shoulders a massive silver dish, in which was heaped what looked like half the cream in Rome; it was decorated more richly than Leo's tiara, with bright red cherries, brown pine kernels, thin green strips of angelica, all kinds of nuts and berries, and was wound about with a great length of dried leaves that had been dipped in gold. The entire assembled company (including myself, I readily admit) drew in its breath.

Strozzi went on, clearly drunk:

"Ah, but all is not what it seems to be, my very dear and *special* friends! No indeed. What you see before you is but the phantasm of the thing itself - the accidents which occlude and conceal the substance, as our good Tomaso d'Aquino would have said. You see, Your Eminences? I am not entirely unversed in the queen of sciences. Excuse me, I digress. Yes, invisible to your eyes, most cherished guests, is a delight more subtle, more - what shall I say, what term to employ? - more *sensuous* (for that must surely be the word!) than the simple sweetness which mere appearances promise. And let me give you a small clue, a tiny hint, so to speak, of the secret which is shortly to be revealed: I provide no implements for this, my final and most exquisite offering; you must use *only your tongues.*"

And with that, he collapsed back in his chair.

The dish was placed somewhat awkwardly in the centre of the table; for some moments we all sat and stared at it. Then Cardinal Salviati stood up, leaned as far as he could across the table, stuck out a greenish, corrugated tongue, and dipped the tip of it into the great mound of cream. He closed his eyes for a moment, licked his lips, then opened his eyes again and nodded.

"Very delicious," he pronounced. "Very delicious indeed. Flavoured with *grappa* and wild honey, if I am not mistaken."

"Bravo, Eminence!" Lorenzo Strozzi cried drunkenly.

Embolded by Salviati's initiative, several of the gentlemen and two of the ladies did likewise; they giggled and nudged each other as they extended their tongues to taste their host's culinary 'apotheosis.' The technique, awkward though it was, was clearly catching on. It fell to Cardinal Ridolfi however, to finally expose the 'secret' of the extraordinary *dolce*; bending across the table and wiggling his tongue, he pushed it into the creamy mass only to withdraw it again with a piercing and womanly shriek.

"*It moved!*" he cried. "God's bones, I tell you it moved! Ah! -"

There was a general commotion as it was observed that the great mound of decorated slop was indeed moving; it shuddered and wiggled, as if suddenly endowed with an alien life of its own. Clotted lumps of cream fell away, nuts and cherries flew off and showered onto the table. It seemed to be *growing*. Ridolfi by now was having an attack of the vapours, wiping his lips furiously with the back of his hand as though he had ingested poison; indeed, had this been a banquet given by Pope Alexander VI Borgia, whose memory still haunted curial slumbers, it might well have been.

Everybody was at the thing now, licking and scraping the cream off as fast as they could; people were stretched out across the table, plates were pushed aside or even fell to the floor; there was screeching and laughing and vulgar gestures. I do not think I have ever seen so many protruding tongues in my life, and it is a spectacle I care never to witness again; human beings look utterly ridiculous with their tongues sticking out. Leo should ban people doing it in all papal states. As a matter of fact, I had entirely forgotten about Leo: he was slumped in his chair, spellbound by the goings on. His eyes bulged and watered.

There was a young woman buried under that grotesque hillock of cream; furthermore, it quickly became obvious, as first a thigh was exposed, then a foot, a wetly glistening pink nipple, and finally a hairy pubic mound, that she was a very naked young woman. The cacophony of screaming and guffawing rapidly swelled in volume as people began to applaud. And still the tongues were at work, probing and wiggling and scraping lasciviously, lingeringly, across the smooth, pale flesh. Two men - one of them rather young for this sort of thing in my opinion - were licking at the same breast, contending for the stiff little nipple, occasionally looking into each other's eyes in a sly, knowing manner as they did so. Much to my surprise however, it was a lady (I use the term cautiously) whose face was buried deep between the shuddering thighs, sucking, slurping shamelessly, her long tongue darting rapidly in and out of the private opening hidden beneath the bush of black hair. I can well imagine what sort of cream she hoped to find down *there*. The young woman stretched herself out in the dish, still half-covered with rapidly liquifying slop; she writhed and groaned and fluttered her eyelids in a sexual ecstasy. The colloidal sludge oozed and squelched beneath her buttocks. Then she uttered a low moan:

"Ah . . . ah!"

The last two things I noticed were that the young man sharing a breast with a fellow diner had drawn out his quivering penis and was rubbing it surreptitiously up against a leg of the table, while the female devotee at the *other* end had pushed a cherry up into the hairy labial glory-hole which was so occupying her attention - presumably for the pleasure of sucking it out again.

"Your Holiness," I said to Leo, "it is time for us to take our leave."

"Yes, you are right, Peppe. Yes, yes."

David Madsen, *Memoirs of a Gnostic Dwarf.*
Dedalus 1995.

David Madsen is also the author of *The Confessions of a Flesheater Cookbook* which will be published by Dedalus in 1996.

CHAPTER 3

THE EDIBLE GALLEON

A meal was hardly a meal in Renaissance Italy, it seems, without a few dozen marzipan goddesses to decorate the table. They brought a note of grace and refinement to the occasion, transforming it from an exercise in stomach-filling to an elevating cultural event.

Decadent cooks go one step further, and make sculptures of the food itself. If life is to be spent in the pursuit of the extravagant, the extreme, the grotesque, the bizarre, then one's diet should reflect the fact. Life, meals, everything must be as artificial as possible - in fact works of art. So why not begin by eating a few statues?

The golden age of food sculpture lasted from about 1500 to the First World War, but there were pioneers before then and it's not entirely forgotten even now. Scraps of the old magnificence survive in the oddest places...

The bakeries of King Stanislas gave birth to the most ingenious fantasies. One day four servants placed on the royal table a huge pie in the shape of a citadel. Suddenly, the lid rose and out of the pie jumped Bébé, the King's dwarf, dressed as a warrior, with a helmet on his head and a pistol in his hand, which he fired, terrifying the ladies.

(MAUGRAS, *LA COUR DE LUNÉVILLE AU XVIIIME SIÈCLE*)

In the last century the Intendant of Gascony gave a magnificent banquet on the birth of the Duke of Burgundy. The centrepiece was covered with wax figures moved by clockwork, which at the conclusion of the feast were set in motion, and gave a representation of the labour of the Dauphiness and the happy birth of an heir to the monarchy.

(E S DALLAS, *KETTNER'S BOOK OF THE TABLE, 1877*)

53

Most extravagant of all is a galley. Its hull is made of forcemeat baked in a specially shaped container. When cooked the meat is unmolded and filled with little birds in a ragout; they in turn are hidden under planking made of veal. From each side of the ship project skewers laden with sweetbreads, cockscombs, meaty bacon, and foies gras. The mast is a larger skewer that flies a cockscomb pennant, and it is festooned with sausage-hung rigging.

(BARBARA KETCHAM WHEATON, *SAVOURING THE PAST*, 1983)

The last familiar example of these ancient ornaments must be the English wedding-cake, the three-tiered ones having, in fact, something in common with the old eighteenth century Chinese temple, which was really a sort of pagoda. It is perhaps some memory of these obsolete conceits which makes chefs produce the inedible fantasies one sees at modern catering exhibitions... the loving representations of Swan Lake in aspic and mutton fat, the Bands of HM Grenadier Guards composed entirely of boiled lobsters...

(SHEILA HUTCHINS, *ENGLISH RECIPES*, 1967)

We start with some simple recipes.

THE MONSTER EGG

(OR BOILED EGG GARGANTUA)

12-24 EGGS

2 VERY CLEAN PIGS' BLADDERS

(ONE SMALL, ONE LARGE)

'Break a dozen or two of eggs, separating the whites from the yolks. Tie up the yolks in a pig's bladder, boil them hard, and take them out again. In a still larger bladder place the whites; into the midst of this put the yolk [it will float to the middle automatically]; tie up the bladder tight; and boil the whole till the white hardens. Uncover the monster egg, and serve it on a bed of spinach or other vegetable. This is a French jest in imitation of the great Madagascar eggs of the Epiornis Maximus, which would contain about twelve dozen hens' eggs.'

(KETTNER'S BOOK OF THE TABLE)

CARPET BAG STEAKS

1 LB (450 G) FILLET STEAK

6 OYSTERS

BUTTER

STRING

Slit the steak to make a pouch and stuff in the oysters. Sew up with string and fry for around 10 minutes each side in butter, quickly at first then more gently. Take the string out of the carpet bag, and serve in the cooking juices, garnished with watercress.

A variation, known as Fillet of Beef Prince of Wales, was created for the young Edward VII. This substitutes pâté de foie gras studded with truffles for the oysters.

CABBIE CLAW

A WIND-SCULPTURE FROM SCOTLAND

A FRESH 2-3 LB COD

A DRAUGHTY PASSAGE

PARSLEY

HORSE RADISH

Skin the cod, and remove the guts. Wash, wipe, sprinkle with salt inside and out. Leave overnight. Next day hang in an open, breezy place but away from the sun (if you can find any) and out of reach of cats. Hang for 48 hours or longer, depending how high you like your cabbie claw to be. Poach in water with parsley and scraped horseradish. Bone, flake and serve with mashed potato and egg sauce, ornamented with parsley and cayenne pepper. The connection with London taxi-drivers is fortuitous, unless you take a cab to the fishmongers to buy your cod.

IÇLI KÖFTE

This is a Turkish dish, sometimes translated as 'crusted meatballs' - which gives a fair idea of the texture but none at all of the possible shapes. Avoid the predictable sphere/sausage morphology, and try making giant olives, small domes, pyramids, buttocks, horses' heads, sphinxes....

3 ONIONS, CHOPPED FINE

1 TABLESPOON PINE NUTS

1LB 10 OZ (750 G) FINELY MINCED LAMB OR BEEF

12 OZ (300 G) BULGUR WHEAT

1 EGG

1 OZ (25 G) CRUSHED WALNUTS

1 TABLESPOON CURRANTS

25 CL OIL

1 TEASPOON SALT

1 TEASPOON PEPPER

1 TEASPOON CUMIN

$^1/_2$ TEASPOON PAPRIKA

A HANDFUL OF PARSLEY, CHOPPED

Brown the onions in oil with the pine nuts. Add half the meat and cook till dry. Take the pan off the heat, and mix the contents with salt, pepper, cumin, walnuts, currants, parsley. This will be the filling for the meatballs. Now for the 'crusted' bit. In a separate bowl mix the bulgur and the remaining meat, then add egg, salt, pepper, paprika. Knead, adding a little water occasionally. Take an egg-sized blob of the resulting mixture, hold it in the palm of your hand and hollow it out with a finger, making the walls as thin as you can. Stuff some filling into this shell, close up and mould with wet hands to what shape you will. Repeat till pan and bowl are empty.

Simmer your creations for 5 minutes in salted water, drain well, then fry in hot oil until brown and crisp.

ROAST HEDGEHOG

There are two ways of doing this. You can use a real hedgehog, or make one of your own. The first recipe comes from Bartolomeo Scappi (chef to the Grand Inquisitor).

PORCHETTO RICCIO

Either skin the hedgehog or remove its bristles with hot water, then extract the innards and roast the animal on the spit or in the oven following the recipe for porcupine [see page 41]. Hedgehog is in season from April to the end of Autumn, but fattest in July and August.

MOCK HEDGEHOG

1 LB EACH OF MINCED BEEF, PORK AND VEAL

8 OZ CHICKEN LIVERS

4 RASHERS UNSMOKED STREAKY BACON

8 OZ MUSHROOMS

1 LARGE ONION, GRATED

10 CRUSHED JUNIPER BERRIES

3 CLOVES GARLIC

1 EGG

SALT, PEPPER

1 TEASPOON EACH THYME, ALLSPICE

2 BAY LEAVES

ROSEMARY

WALNUT HALVES

1 BLACK OLIVE

Chop the mushrooms and chicken livers very finely and fry them softly for 5 minutes. Leave to cool. Combine the minced meat in a bowl with the onion, garlic, juniper berries, thyme, allspice, salt & pepper, egg, mushrooms and chicken livers. Mix. Transfer to a roasting tin, adding a little oil if the mince is very lean. Sculpt the mixture to look like a hedgehog. Stripe the beast with bacon and

bay leaves, and stud with nuts. Use pieces of olive for eyes and
nose. Scatter some rosemary over its back. Roast in a hot oven for
15 minutes, then in a medium oven for another 75 minutes. Serve
in its own gravy.

No Holds Barred
(Rôti Sans Pareil)

This is a more ambitious dish, which we first encountered in *Venus
in the Kitchen* by Norman Douglas, who says he took it from A T
Raimbault's *Le Parfait Cuisinier*. The recipe was also found among
the papers of Grimod de la Reynière, who added comparisons of
the birds' tender flesh to the complexions of famous actresses. It
requires a special combination of dexterity and brute strength - but
no 'sculpting' as such.

1 CAPER	1 QUAIL	1 CHICKEN*
1 ANCHOVY	A FEW VINE	1 DUCK*
A FEW DROPS OF	LEAVES	1 GOOSE*
OIL	1 GOLDEN	1 TURKEY
1 LARGE OLIVE**	PLOVER*	1 BUSTARD*
1 BECCAFICO OR	1 LAPWING*	
GARDEN	1 PARTRIDGE*	* BONED
WARBLER*	1 WOODCOCK*	** STONED
1 ORTOLAN	1 TEAL*	
1 LARK*	1 PHEASANT	
1 THRUSH*	1 GUINEA-FOWL*	

Make a paste of the anchovy and caper, and stuff the olive with it. Then, proceeding in order down the list, stuff each ingredient into the one below. Put the assembled 'thing' into a big pot with a clove-studded onion, some pieces of ham, bacon, celery, carrots, coriander seeds, garlic, salt and pepper. Seal down the lid with pastry and cook in a slow oven for ten hours. Serve with chips and frozen peas.

Cyril Connolly, in *Shade Those Laurels,* gives a similar recipe, but says it should be cooked for 24 hours, not 10. He adds this serving suggestion:

'Now listen carefully - we're getting to the holy of holies of cooking! We have here the quintessence of forest, marsh, plain and farmyard, all these juices and emanations are being stealthily volatilised and united and blended into the most exquisite whole, a unique gastronomic experience - but meanwhile this quintessence has penetrated to the very heart of the whole matter, that is to the olive. So you carve open the bustard very carefully and throw it out of the window or give it to the dogs if you have any; same treatment for the turkey, the goose,... the chicken, the guinea-fowl, the teal, the woodcock, the partridge, the plover, the quail, the ortolan, the poor little beccafico, until finally in a spirit of true gratitude and admiration we serve ... the olive.'

KAROLY ECLAIRS

This is a trick recipe, guaranteed to please. Make some éclair cases with choux pastry. Cook some liver of game, then mash and mix with bechamel and cream. Inject this purée into the éclairs and cover them with bitter chocolate sauce.

THE SURPRISE

This is a variation on Newfoundland Pork Cake. Excellent with vodka, sherry, or plum brandy c 2am.

24 OZ SALT OR PICKLED PORK, MINCED

3 CUPS FLOUR

1 TEASPOON EACH OF GROUND CLOVES, GINGER, CINNAMON,

NUTMEG

GRATED RIND OF A LEMON

1 LB CURRANTS

1 LB SEEDLESS RAISINS

8 OZ CHOPPED WALNUTS

8 OZ CANDIED PEEL

2 CUPS BLACK TREACLE

$^1/_2$ CUP RUM

2 TEASPOONS BAKING POWDER

3 EGGS

Stand the pork in a warm place for 30 minutes, then mix it with the rest of the ingredients except the eggs. Separate the egg yolks from the whites. Stir in the yolks. Beat the whites to a stiff foam and fold them in to the mixture. Bake in a cool to moderate oven for 3 hours.

LE CLUB DES HACHICHINS

by Théophile Gautier

One evening in December, obeying a mysterious invitation couched in enigmatic terms intelligible only to initiates, I travelled to a distant part of the city, a kind of oasis of solitude in the centre of Paris, which the river seems to defend with its encircling arms from the molestations of civilization. It was an old house in the Ile Saint-Louis, Hôtel Pimodan, built by Lauzun, where a bizarre club that I had recently joined held its monthly meetings, which I was about to attend for the first time.

Although it was only six o'clock, the night was already dark. The fog, made thicker by the proximity to the Seine, blurred every detail with its ragged veils, punctured at various distances by the reddish glow of lanterns and bars of light escaping from illuminated windows. The road was soaked with rain, and glittered under the street-lamps like a lake reflecting strings of lights. A bitter wind, heavy with icy particles, whipped at my face, its howling forming the high notes of a symphony whose bass was played by the swollen waves crashing into the piers of the bridges below. The evening lacked none of winter's rough poetry.

It was hard to pick out the house from the mass of sombre buildings along that deserted quay; but my coachman, standing in his seat, managed to read the faded gilt lettering on a marble plaque. This was the place where the adepts met...

I rang the bell. The door was opened with the usual precautions, and I found myself in a large room lit at the far end by a few lamps. Walking in was like stepping back two centuries. Time, which passes so quickly, seemed to have stood still in that house; like a clock which someone has forgotten to wind, it was stuck perpetually at the same date.

The walls were lined in white-painted wood, half-panelled with cloth stained brown with age; on the gigantic stove stood a statue which might once have belonged in a garden alley at Versailles. On the domed ceiling was a painted allegory in the overblown style of Lemoine; indeed it may well have been one of his works.

I moved towards the lighted end of the room, where a

number of human forms stood excitedly round a table. As I entered the circle of light, a cheer of recognition burst from them, stirring the sonorous depths of the ancient building.

"Here he is! Here he is!" cried several voices at once. "Let him have his share!"

The doctor was standing at a sideboard, where a tray of tiny Japanese saucers had been placed, each with a gilded silver spoon. Dipping a spatula into a crystal vase, the doctor scooped out a piece of greenish paste or jelly, about the size of a thumb, onto each saucer.

The doctor's face shone with enthusiasm, his eyes glittered, his cheekbones flared, the veins on his forehead stood out, his dilated nostrils sucked in the air in powerful draughts.

"This" he said, handing me my dose, "will be deducted from your portion of paradise."

When everyone had eaten his share, coffee was served in the Arabian style - with grounds and no sugar. Then we sat down to eat.

This inversion of culinary habits will undoubtedly surprise the reader; it is hardly the custom to have coffee before the soup, and jelly is usually taken as a dessert. An explanation is in order.

In the Orient in times gone by there existed a redoubtable sect commanded by a sheikh known as the Old Man of the Mountains, or Prince of the Assassins.

This Old Man was unquestioningly obeyed. His subjects, the Assassins, carried out his orders with absolute devotion. No danger could stop them, even certain death. At a sign from their chief they would hurl themselves from a tower or stab a sovereign in his palace in the midst of his guards.

What means did the Old Man of the Mountains use to obtain such obedience? He had in his possession the recipe for a marvellous drug, which was capable of producing the most dazzling hallucinations. Those who tasted it, on waking from their intoxicated states, found real life so sad and colourless that they would joyfully make any sacrifice to return to the paradise of their dreams; if a man was killed in the course of obeying the sheikh's orders he went straight to heaven - or, if he survived, was allowed to partake once again of the happiness conveyed by the mysterious drug.

The green paste doled out by the doctor was precisely this substance: that is to say, *hashish*, whence *hashishin*, or eater of *hashish*, which is the root of the word *assassin*, a term whose ferocious connotations are easily explained by the sanguinary habits of the Old Man's followers...

The meal was served in a most bizarre manner, in all sorts of extravagant and picturesque vessels.

Large Venetian goblets veined with milky spirals, German tankards inscribed with mottoes and legends, Flemish stoneware jugs, narrow-necked flasks still wrapped in straw - these were our glasses, bottles and carafes.

The opaque porcelain of Louis Lebeut, as well as English china prettily decorated with flowers, were both striking in their absence. No two plates were the same, each one had its own particular merit. China, Japan and Saxony each contributed samples of their finest clays and richest colours. It was all a little chipped, a little cracked, but in exquisite taste.

The serving dishes were mostly faience from Limoges or enamels from Bernard de Palissy. Sometimes, beneath the food, a carver's knife would encounter a porcelain reptile, frog or bird. The edible eel mixed its coils with those of the moulded viper.

A simple-hearted philistine would have felt a certain alarm at the sight of these hairy, bearded, moustachioed guests, some with the most unusual hairstyles, brandishing their 16th century daggers, Malaysian kriss or navajas, bent over their food which the guttering flames of the lamps cast into the most suspicious-looking shapes.

As the dinner drew to an end some of the more fervent members began to feel the effects of the green paste. I was already experiencing a complete transposition of tastes. The water I was drinking seemed to me a most exquisite wine, the meat turned to raspberries in my mouth, the raspberries into meat. I could not have distinguished a cutlet from a peach.

My neighbours began to look rather odd; great owl-sized

pupils stared at me; noses stretched in probosces; mouths widened into sleigh-bell slits. Faces were tinted with unnatural colours. One man, a pale visage in a black beard, cackled loudly at an invisible comedy; another made incredible efforts to raise his glass to his lips, his contortions provoking deafening shouts of laughter. A man next to me was shaken by nervous spasms, and whirled his thumbs at fantastic speed. Another slumped back in his chair, eyes glazed, arms limp, floating voluptuously on a bottomless sea of annihilation.

With my elbows on the table I contemplated this scene in the light of my remaining reason, which guttered fitfully like a candle about to go out. Dull shudders of heat passed through my body, and madness, like a wave that foams round a rock and draws back before flinging itself forward again, entered and left my brain, finally invading it completely. Hallucination, that strange guest, had come to stay...

Théophile Gautier, 'Le Club des Hachichins', *Revue des Deux Mondes*, 1846.

CHAPTER 4

THE GASTRONOMIC
MAUSOLEUM

One morning in February 1783 a card arrived at the houses of various Parisian notables. The card was bordered in black and bore a picture of a sarcophagus surmounted by a crucifix.

> *The pleasure of your company is requested at the funeral procession and burial of a banquet to be given by Messire Alexandre-Balthasar-Laurent Grimod de la Reynière, equerry and parliamentary advocate, drama correspondent of the Journal de Neuchâtel, at his house on the Champs Elysées. Guests will assemble at 9 o'clock and supper will be served at 10 o'clock.*

Grimod de la Reynière, one of the great gourmets of 18th century France and editor of the *Almanach des Gourmands,* not only invited guests to this dinner, but 300 spectators as well. When the guests arrived, they found the dining room draped in black. The centrepiece of the table was a sarcophagus, and the proceedings were a grim theatrical joke. One course consisted of nothing but pork dishes, which Grimod proudly announced to have been supplied by a member of his family. This shocking revelation of low social connections was untrue (although his grandfather had been a pork butcher and notorious glutton), but Grimod's aim was to humiliate his arrogant mother by pointing out where her family had made its money. His parents were duly offended and had him exiled from Paris. He took his revenge a few years later with a second funeral dinner, where the pork-trade theme was even more heavily underlined: the black velvet hangings on the walls were embroidered with symbols of charcuterie, and the ivory handles of the cutlery were carved in the shape of pigs.

This meal was almost certainly the model for another black meal - that given by Jean Des Esseintes in Huysmans' novel, *A Rebours*.

The dining room, draped in black, opened onto a garden swiftly transformed for the occasion. The paths had been dusted with charcoal, the ornamental pond filled with ink and edged with black basalt, and the shrubberies replanted with cypresses and pines. The black tablecloth on which dinner was served was decorated with baskets of violets and scabious. Tapers flickered in chandeliers and green-flamed candelabra cast a strange glow.

To the accompaniment of a hidden orchestra playing funeral marches, guests were waited on by negresses, naked but for slippers and silver stockings embroidered with tears.

The guests ate off black-bordered plates and enjoyed turtle soup, rye bread from Russia, black olives from Turkey, caviare, mullet botargo, black pudding from Frankfurt, game served with sauces the colour of liquorice and boot-polish, truffle purées, chocolate creams, plum puddings, nectarines, black grape jellies, mulberries and dark-fleshed cherries. They drank wines from Limagne and Roussillon, Tenedos, Valdepeñas and Oporto out of glasses tinted black. After coffee and walnut cordial, the evening was brought to a close with kvass, porter and stout.

On the invitations, which looked like funeral announcements, the dinner was described as a memorial banquet for the host's virility, lately but only temporarily deceased.

Grimod de la Reynière, however, was not the first to combine the banquet and the grave. Cassius Dio relates just such an occasion when Domitian entertained various senators and nobles. In the dining room walls and furnishings were all in black. At each guest's place his name had been carved onto a *stele,* or grave marker. They were treated to a frightening dance performed by naked boys painted black and offered food normally presented at sacrifices for the dead. None of the terrified guests dared to talk during the meal, and the Emperor spoke of nothing but killing and death. It was with great relief that they were allowed to return home.

DEATH ON THE NILE

If you're planning a *fête macabre* give some serious thought to location. Setting is all important. The necropolis of Sakkara in Egypt would be most appropriate. There you could find a suitable 2nd dynasty tomb and reproduce this menu, provided for an Egyptian Princess who was buried about 3000 B.C.

A TRIANGULAR LOAF OF BREAD MADE FROM EMMER
WHEAT ON A POTTERY DISH.

BARLEY PORRIDGE ON AN ALABASTER DISH.

A COOKED FISH, CLEANED AND HEADLESS.

A PIGEON STEW.

A COOKED QUAIL (CLEANED AND DRESSED WITH THE
HEAD TUCKED UNDER ONE WING).

TWO COOKED KIDNEYS.

RIBS AND LEGS OF BEEF.

STEWED FIGS, IN A POTTERY BOWL.

NABK BERRIES (SIMILAR TO CHERRIES, FROM SIDDER)
IN A DIORITE BOWL.

CIRCULAR CAKES SWEETENED WITH HONEY.

SMALL JARS PACKED WITH CHEESE.

WINE IN A LARGE JAR.

Ideally, of course, the princess will return from the dead to share it with you. Especially if the meal is preceded by a cocktail - 2 parts brandy, 1 part calvados, 1 part sweet vermouth - vulgarly known as a 'corpse reviver'.

Another suitable location is Death Row at the State Prison in Washington, where the murderer Thomas Grasso was executed in January 1995. With the agreement of the authorities, one might re-enact Grasso's final meal, which consisted of mussels, scallops, tinned spaghetti served at room temperature, and a double hamburger. Should the prison authorities prove unco-operative, there is no reason why the meal should not be prepared at home. At a little additional expense, replica electric chairs (in which many a goose has been cooked) could be provided for the guests. Some people might find this idea tasteless however. The thought of having reproduction furniture in their house is too awful to contemplate. So here's another suggestion for one of those deft little finishing touches that make the difference between a meal and an Experience: garnish with syringes filled with cyanide, arranged on swabs of cotton wool and served on kidney dishes by men in white coats.

Of course most of us are far too busy to go off to Sakkara or Washington for dinner, so here are some humbler dishes for everyday decadence.

GRAVLAX

(LITERALLY, 'BURIED' OR 'GRAVE' SALMON)

————•◆•————

The best way to prepare gravlax is to send someone extremely rugged and bold to Scandanavia in early winter. There they should dig a hole in the soft sandy earth on the shore of a lake and bury a salmon in it, sandwiched between two layers of birch twigs and fir branches weighted down with stones and covered with earth. The wooden cross is optional. The salmon has to be left for three to six days before it is ready to eat. (Alternatively it can be left for between six and twelve weeks by which time the flesh will have fermented). Of course, burying a fish for three days before resurrecting and eating it can be interpreted as a blasphemous parody of Christian ritual - but as we said, the wooden cross is optional.

If you don't know any outdoor types you can make gravlax in the comfort of your own fitted kitchen like this.

3 - 4 LB SALMON, FILLETED, SKIN ON

A BIG BUNCH OF DILL

CURE FOR THE SALMON, MADE WITH:

4 TSP BLACK PEPPERCORNS, ROUGHLY CRUSHED

4 TBSP SALT

2 TBSP HONEY

2 TBSP BRANDY

Wash and dry the salmon. Mix the pepper, salt, honey and brandy. Lay half the dill on a long dish, then half the salmon, skin side down. Rub in half the cure. Add the remaining dill. Rub the rest of the cure into the flesh of the other half of the salmon. Lay it over the first half, skin side up, cover with foil and put some weights on top. Stick the whole thing in the fridge for 48 hours, and turn every 12 hours.

When it's ready, dress with a sweet mustard and dill mayonnaise (2 egg yolks, 300 ml of olive oil, lemon juice, 4 tbsp French mustard, 2 tbsp sugar, 2 tbsp dill), made in the usual way.

For real cheats, there's also the gravlax which comes ready-entombed in vacuum-packs at supermarkets. Resurrect the corpse as delicately as possible and decorate extravagantly.

SOLES IN COFFINS

For this Victorian recipe you should ideally use black sole instead of white. The ingredients are as follows:

1 LARGE POTATO PER PERSON

1 PINT OF BÉCHAMEL SAUCE

2 FILLETS OF SOLE PER PERSON

HALF A LOBSTER CUT INTO $^1/_2$ INCH PIECES

8 COOKED PRAWNS PER PERSON. KEEP THEM HOT

$^1/_4$ LB BUTTON MUSHROOMS

SLICES OF TRUFFLE

BUTTER AND MILK

A LITTLE DOUBLE CREAM

$^1/_4$ BOTTLE OF WHITE WINE

Preheat the oven to gas mark 6, 400° F, and bake the potatoes in their jackets. Slice the potatoes lengthways and carefully remove their insides, leaving the skins in their original shape. Keep the skins warm, but do not let them dry out. Reserve the insides.

Whip into the Béchamel sauce a tablespoon of grated Parmesan cheese and $^1/_4$ lb of softened butter. Keep the sauce warm.

Roll the soles and poach them in white wine for 10 minutes. Add the lobster to poach for the last five minutes. Keep hot.

Slice the mushrooms finely and sauté them in butter. Keep hot.

Pour the sauce into the potato skins until they are about one third full. Drain the fillets and stand them in the sauce. Add the lobster, prawns and mushrooms. Cover the fillets with any sauce which is left. If there is none, use the cream. Arrange on a flat ovenproof serving dish and put in the oven for 5 minutes.

Meanwhile, mash the potato with milk and butter and season with salt and pepper. When the potato coffins come out of the oven arrange the mashed potato in piles around them. Put 3 slices of truffle on top of the coffins and serve immediately.

It occurs to me that there really ought to be a place in this meal for the worm - that little creature so beloved of the decadent poets. If your guests don't like the idea of tucking into a plate of worms, try reminding them that not only is this creature an excellent source of protein, but that here is their opportunity to eat the worm before the worm eats them. They should think of it as a pre-emptive act of revenge.

The French anthropologist Gontran de Poncins, who lived with Netsilik Eskimos in 1938-9, describes a caribou hunt in his book *Kabloona* where his hosts, after skinning their prey, start eating the yellow-eyed parasitic worms that live in the flesh. *'Kailek squeezed the worms out with his thumb and popped them into his mouth. I, who was determined to try everything once, took one up, shut my eyes, and put it in my mouth. It was sweetish, inside its surprisingly fuzzy, raspberry-like skin, and I spat out the skin and had another, while Kailek sat with a heap of them before him on the snow.'*

If you can't get a good maggoty piece of caribou, serve Italian *vermicelli* ('little worms') in a suitably gruesome sauce, such as squid in its own ink.

1LB FRESH SQUID WITH INK-SACS INTACT

OLIVE OIL

GARLIC

PARSLEY

WHITE WINE

GINGER AND CHILLI TO TASTE (OR NOT AT ALL)

Clean the squid as follows: pull the head out of the body, and chop off and reserve the tentacles above the eyes. (Try not to meet their melancholy gaze as you do it. They have a way of haunting your dreams.) Then carefully empty out the dribbly yellow and cream innards and the transparent bone from the pouch-shaped body; among these you'll find an exquisite little silver sac containing the ink. Put this in a strainer. Wash and skin the body pouch and slice into rings or squares. Fry the tentacles and body in olive oil and garlic, then add a glass of white wine and a handful of parsley. Holding the strainer over the pan, crush the ink sacs with a spoon, then wash through with wine or cooking liquids. Don't crush the sacs between your fingers unless you want to look like an apprentice printer and smell of fish for the next two days. The ink is extraordinarily black, thick and greasy.

Cook the squid for ten minutes, then mix with the boiled vermicelli and serve.

KOLIVA

This is a sweet specially prepared for the dead in Greece. It is probably a modern variant on an Ancient Greek dish mentioned by Aristophanes called Polyspermia.

500 G (1LB) WHOLE WHEAT

THREE PINCHES OF SALT

120G (4OZ) SMALL CURRANTS

120G (4OZ) RAISINS

120G (4OZ) COARSELY CHOPPED WALNUTS

150G (5OZ) SHELLED AND FLAKED ALMONDS

1 POMEGRANATE, SHELLED AND SEEDED

1 TSP GROUND CINNAMON

1 TSP GROUND CORIANDER

1 TSP GROUND CUMIN

TOPPING:

500G (1LB) PLAIN FLOUR

500G (1LB) CASTER SUGAR

10 SUGARED ALMONDS

HANDFUL OF RAISINS

Remove any impurities from the wheat. Dispose of the impurities in the sea. Rinse the wheat three times and pour the water on a tree or plant. Soak wheat overnight. Strain, cover with water, add three pinches of salt and boil until tender. Strain and spread the wheat out on a clean tablecloth to dry overnight.

Light a candle and bring to mind the dead for whom this dish is being prepared.

Gently mix the dry wheat with the other ingredients. Spread out on flat trays. Roast the flour dry in a frying pan turning continuously with a spatula until golden brown. Allow to cool. Spread a thin layer of flour on top of the wheat and press down lightly. Sprinkle a little sugar on top and press down again with a piece of paper. Decorate with sugared almonds, raisins, pomegranate seeds and/or ground cinnamon.

PERYS COFYNS

(PEAR COFFINS)

———•◦•———

This is a more bizarre dessert which dates from the Middle Ages.

10 HARD PEARS

JUICE OF 3 LEMONS

CINNAMON

$^1/_2$ CUP OF LENTILS

1 SMALL STALK OF CELERY

$^1/_2$ TEASPOON OF SALT

$^1/_4$ CUP OF FINELY CHOPPED DATES

$^1/_2$ TEASPOON OF DRIED SWEET BASIL

1 CUP OF BEEF BROTH

1 CUP OF RASPBERRIES

1 TABLESPOON OF HONEY

Preheat oven to 350°.

Cut the pears in half lengthways. Carefully remove the stalk and core. Coat the pears in lemon juice and sprinkle lightly with cinnamon. Bake in the oven for about five to ten minutes. This should turn the pears from hard to firm. Do not let them go soft. Put to one side to cool.

Wash the lentils and put into a casserole with the celery, finely chopped, salt, finely chopped dates, basil and beef broth. Bring to the boil and cook over a very low heat for about fifteen to twenty minutes. Add boiling water if necessary to prevent sticking. Put raspberries, honey and $1/4$ of a cup and 1 tablespoon of water into a pot. Bring quickly to the boil. Remove immediately and allow to cool.

Scoop one tablespoon of lentils into each of the pear coffins and top with a tablespoon of raspberry.

I know it's customary to serve coffee at the end of a meal, but I suggest in this case that cocoa from Caracas should be offered. This is on the basis of the entry on 'cocoa' from Alexandre Dumas *père*'s Dictionnaire. He writes:

" It is the practice to 'earth' cocoa in the ground, in order to make it lose its bitterness; and one must be careful, before using it, to get rid of this cover of earth, which makes it a bit musty. This does not prevent the cocoa of Caracas, the only one subjected to this preparatory burial, from producing the best of all known chocolate."

And to accompany the cocoa? A Mexican pastry in the form of a skeleton perhaps? And a reading . . .

The Odyssey

by Homer

"Now when we had gone down to the ship and to the sea, first of all we drew the ship unto the fair salt water, and placed the mast and sails in the black ship, and took those sheep and put them therein, and ourselves too climbed on board, sorrowing, and shedding big tears. And in the wake of our dark-prowed ship she sent a favouring wind that filled the sails, a kindly escort, — even Circe of the braided tresses, a dread goddess of human speech. And we set in order all the gear throughout the ship and sat us down; and the wind and the helmsman guided our barque. And all day long her sails were stretched in her seafaring; and the sun sank and all the ways were darkened.

"She came to the limits of the world, to the deep-flowing Oceanus. There is the land and the city of the Cimmerians, shrouded in mist and cloud, and never does the shining sun look down on them with his rays, neither when he climbs up the starry heavens, nor when again he turns earthward from the firmament, but deadly night is outspread over miserable mortals. Thither we came and ran the ship ashore and took out the sheep; but for our part we held on our way along the stream of Oceanus, till we came to the place which Circe had declared to us.

"There Perimedes and Eurylochus held the victims, but I drew my sharp sword from my thigh, and dug a pit, as it were a cubit in length and breadth, and about it poured a drink-offering to all the dead, first with the mead and thereafter with sweet wine, and for the third time with water. And I sprinkled white meal thereon, and entreated with many prayers the strengthless heads of the dead, and promised that on my return to Ithaca I would offer in my halls a barren heifer, the best I had, and fill the pyre with treasure, and apart unto Teiresias alone sacrifice a black ram without spot, the fairest of my flock. But when I had besought the tribes of the dead with vows and prayers, I took the sheep and cut their throats over the trench, and the dark blood flowed forth, and lo, the spirits of the dead that be departed gathered them from out of Erebus. Brides and youths unwed, and old men of many and evil days, and tender maidens with grief yet fresh at heart; and many there were, wounded with bronze-shod spears, men slain in fight with their bloody mail about them. And these many ghosts flocked together from every side about the trench with a wondrous cry, and pale fear gat hold on me. Then did I speak to my company and command them to flay the sheep that lay slain by the pitiless sword, and to consume them with fire, and to make prayer to the gods, to mighty Hades and to dread Persephone, and myself I drew the sharp sword from my thigh and sat there, suffering not the strengthless heads of the dead to draw nigh to the blood, ere I had word of Teiresias.

"And first came the soul of Elpenor, my companion, that had not yet been buried beneath the wide-way earth; for we left the corpse behind us in the hall of Circe, unwept and unburied, seeing that another task was instant on us. At the sight of him I wept and had compassion on him, and uttering my voice spake to him winged words: 'Elpenor, how has thou come beneath the darkness and the shadow? Thou has come fleeter on foot than I in my black ship.' "

"So spake I, and with a moan he answered me, saying: 'Son of Laertes, of the seed of Zeus, Odysseus of many devices, an evil doom of some god was my bane and wine out of measure. When I laid me down on the house-top of Circe I minded me not to descend again by the way of the tall ladder, but fell right down from the roof, and my neck was broken off from the bones of the spine, and my spirit went down to the house of Hades. And now I pray thee in the name of those whom we left, who are no more with us, thy wife, and thy sire who cherished thee when as yet thou wert a little one, and Telemachus, whom thou didst leave in thy halls alone; forasmuch as I know that on thy way hence from out the dwelling of Hades, thou wilt stay thy well-wrought ship at the isle Aeaean, even then, my lord, I charge thee to think on me. Leave me not unwept and unburied as thou goest hence, nor turn thy back upon me, lest haply I bring on thee the anger of the gods. Nay, burn me there with mine armour, all that is mine, and pile me a barrow on the shore of the grey sea, the grave of a luckless man, that even men unborn may hear my story. Fulfil me this and plant upon the barrow mine oar, wherewith I rowed in the days of my life, while yet I was among my fellows.' "

"Even so he spake, and I answered him saying: "All this, luckless man, will I perform for thee and do."

"Even so we twain were sitting holding sad discourse, I on the one side, stretching forth my sword over the blood, while on the other side the ghost of my friend told all his tale.

"Anon came up the soul of my mother dead, Anticleia, the daughter of Autolycus the great-hearted, whom I left alive when I departed for sacred Ilios. At the sight of her I wept, and was moved with compassion, yet even so, for all my sore grief, I suffered her not to draw nigh to the blood, ere I had word of Teiresias.

"Anon came the soul of Theban Teiresias, with a golden sceptre in his hand, and he knew me and spake unto me: 'Son of Laertes, of the seed of Zeus, Odysseus of many devices, what seekest thou *now*, wretched man, wherefore hast thou left the sunlight and come hither to behold the dead and a land desolate of joy? Nay, hold off from the ditch and draw back thy sharp sword, that I may drink of the blood and tell thee sooth.' "

"So spake he and I put up my silver-studded sword into the sheath, and when he had drunk the dark blood, even then did the noble seer speak unto me, saying: 'Thou art asking of thy sweet returning, great Odysseus, but that will the god make hard for thee; for methinks thou shalt not pass unheeded by the Shaker of the Earth, who hath laid up wrath in his heart against thee, for rage at the blinding of his dear son. Yet even so, through many troubles, ye may come home, if thou wilt restrain thy spirit and the spirit of thy men so soon as thou shalt bring thy well-wrought ship nigh to the isle Thrinacia, fleeing the sea of violet blue, when ye find the herds of Helios grazing and his brave flocks, of Helios who overseeth all and overheareth all things. If thou doest these no hurt, being heedful of thy return, so may ye yet reach Ithaca, albeit in evil case. But if thou hurtest them, I foreshow ruin for thy ship and for thy men, and even though thou shalt thyself escape, late shalt thou return in evil plight, with the loss of all thy company, on board the ship of strangers, and thou shalt find sorrows in thy house, even proud men that devour thy living, while they woo thy godlike wife and offer the gifts of wooing. Yet I tell thee, on thy coming thou shalt avenge their violence. But when thou hast slain the wooers in thy halls, whether by guile, or openly with the edge of the sword, thereafter go thy way, taking with thee a shapen oar, till thou shalt come to such men as know not the sea, neither eat meat savoured with salt; yea, nor have they knowledge of ships of purple cheek, nor shapen oars which serve for wings to ships. And I will give thee a most manifest token, which cannot escape thee. In the day when another wayfarer shall meet thee and say that thou hast a winnowing fan on thy stout shoulder, even then make fast thy shapen oar in the earth and do goodly sacrifice to the lord Poseidon, even with a ram and a bull and a boar, the mate of swine, and depart for home and offer holy hecatombs to the deathless gods that keep the wide heaven, to each in order due. And from the sea shall thine own death come, the gentlest death that may be, which shall end thee foredone with smooth old age, and the folk shall dwell happily around thee.' "

Homer, *The Odyssey*, Book XI (transl. Butcher & Lang).

CHAPTER 5

BLOOD, THE VITAL
INGREDIENT

The Marquise had gone from doctor to doctor - seeking out the celebrated and the obscure, the empirically-inclined and the homeopathic - but at every turn she had been met with a sad shake of the head. Only one of them had taken it upon himself to indicate a possible remedy: Rosaria (the Marquise' daughter) must join the ranks of consumptives who go at dawn to the abattoirs to drink the lukewarm blood freshly drawn from the calves which are bled to make veal.

On the first few occasions, the marquise had taken it upon herself to lead the child down into the abattoirs; but the horrid odour of the blood, the warm carcasses, the bellowing of the beasts as they came to be slaughtered, the carnage of the butchering … all that had caused her terrible anguish and had sickened her heart. She could not stand it.

Rosaria had been less intimidated. She had bravely swallowed the lukewarm blood, saying only: "This red milk is a little thick for my taste."

JEAN LORRAIN, *THE GLASS OF BLOOD*

Coming as it does from the decadent pen of Jean Lorrain, this story might seem little more than the perverse outpourings of a particularly overheated imagination. But an illustration from the magazine *Le Monde Illustré* of 1890 shows precisely this scene. A well-heeled young Parisian woman is standing in the courtyard of the slaughterhouse at La Villette. All about her is carnage. Nearby, a slaughterman, meat cleaver in hand, stands over the body of a freshly despatched cow. The woman, meanwhile, sips delicately from her glass, while others, similarly demure, wait patiently by the gate to receive their portion.

This puts one in mind of a favourite figure of the Decadent imagination - the Vampire. In Decadent poetry, the vampire is often used as a metaphor for the poet's mistress. She sucks the lifeblood and vitality out of him, leaving him dull and listless. For this he curses her and wishes her dead, but she has an appalling power over him, from which he can never break free.

Although the vampire has come down to us as a male character, loosely based on the Romanian king Vlad Dracul, alias Vlad the Impaler, it seems more probable that the original vampire was a woman - the 17th century Hungarian Countess, Elisabeth de Báthory.

The Countess occupied the castle of Csejthe and belonged to one of the most powerful families in Hungary. She was a vain, sadistic and thoroughly debauched woman, who took delight in pinching the flesh of her serving girls with special silver pincers. Her husband may have curbed some of her more depraved practices, but after his death in 1604, she went on an orgy of blood-letting. By now she was forty three years old and her once considerable beauty was fading rapidly. The creams, lotions, magic herbs and spells were of no avail in this struggle with nature and the Countess was becoming obsessed with her loss. One day, she slapped a chambermaid so hard that blood from the girl's nose splattered the Countess's face. On washing it off, she became convinced that where the blood had splashed her, the skin was whiter and less wrinkled than before. Given the properties that had been ascribed to blood in medicine, alchemy and witchcraft, the Countess reasoned that virgins' blood would be the substance to restore her lost youth.

With the aid of a sinister old peasant woman named Dorotta Szentes, the Countess began procuring and murdering young peasant girls. They were drained of their blood, which was warmed, and, just before dawn, the Countess would lower herself into a bath of it. She is also said to have drunk the blood of young girls she was torturing, and there was talk of cannibalism at the castle.

Before long, Countess Elisabeth was requiring at least five serving girls a week to satisfy her terrible obsession, and in order for her sadistic activities to remain undetected for so long must have required considerable complicity on the part of the local people. The local Lutheran pastor, for example, was sometimes having to bury up to nine mutilated bodies a night in the village church-yard.

Unfortunately, the Countess's blood-bath was not having

the desired effect. Her beauty was not being restored. A local woman with a knowledge of the black arts explained that this was because peasant blood was of inferior quality. Only noble blood had the restorative properties the Countess required. In the winter of 1609 she began taking into her home the daughters of the minor aristocracy under the cover of instructing them in the social graces. The disappearance of these unfortunate girls however became far more difficult to explain than that of peasants' daughters. The Countess was denounced after the naked bodies of four of them were found at the foot of the castle walls.

Elisabeth de Báthory is said to have been responsible for the deaths of up to six hundred and fifty girls, but it required an act of Parliament to have her arrested. Even then her social position protected her from being brought to trial. Instead, her cousin, the Lord Palatine of Hungary, ordered that she be walled up in a tiny room in her own castle. She was fed through a small hatch and survived in this way for three and half years.

The consumption of blood doesn't always have such a bestial aspect to it. The Irish, among others, used to make a sort of blood cake whereby a layer of blood was left to coagulate and then sprinkled with salt. A second layer of liquid was added and also left to coagulate. In this way a block was formed which was then cut up into squares and put aside as food for use in times of scarcity.

Another blood 'recipe' from Ireland is mentioned by the early 18th century traveller, Henri Misson de Valbourg. In his *Memoirs and Observations in his Travels over England translated by Mr Ozell*, he notes that the peasants "bleed their cows and boil the blood with some of the milk and butter which came from the same beasts, and this with a mixture of savoury herbs, is one of their most delicious dishes." It is difficult to gauge the degree of irony in that last remark.

Blood makes an excellent basis for a Decadent meal. Dark, heavy, rich and sinister, it combines beautifully with other Decadent themes: vice, corruption, incest and death.

To start the meal we suggest a black blood soup from Sweden.

Svartsoppa

For the meat and giblets:

Giblets of 1 goose (heart, gizzard,
neck, head, wing tips, feet and liver)
1 - 1^1/$_2$ litres of water
Tablespoon of salt
1 slice of yellow or red onion
4 - 6 white peppercorns
2 - 4 cloves

For the soup:

6 decilitres of goose or pig's blood
3^1/$_2$ litres mixture of bouillon (a good meat stock,
light or dark) and giblet stock
3 tablespoons of butter
7 - 9 tablespoons of flour
3 teaspoons salt
6 - 7 tablespoons granulated sugar
^{1}/$_2$ teaspoon white pepper
^{1}/$_2$ teaspoon of ginger
^{1}/$_2$ teaspoon ground cloves
Red currant jelly
4 - 6 teaspoons distilled vinegar
1 decilitre cognac
1 - 3 decilitres of red wine, dry madeira, dry sherry or port

For the garnish

GOOSE GIBLETS AND MEAT

5 - 6 GOOD SOUR APPLES

24 PRUNES

$^1/_2$ LITRE WATER

2 - 3 TABLESPOONS SUGAR

GOOSE LIVER SAUSAGE

Wash the giblets thoroughly. Put them in cold water and bring to the boil slowly. Skim and add the onions and spices. Bring back to the boil and cook gently for 2 - 3 hours until the meat is well done. Strain and leave the stock to cool. Skim thoroughly when cold. When cool cut the giblets into regular pieces and remove all the bones.

Wash the prunes and soak in water for a while. Wash, peel, core, halve and then slice the apples. Heat the sugar and water together, in which mixture the apples are then cooked, a few at a time. Remove and set them aside. Stone the prunes and cook in the same way, reserving the resultant fruit stock.

Strain the blood. Melt the butter, add the flour and stir until cooked. Add the bouillon and giblet stock mixture and allow to cook slowly for 10 minutes. Strain and return to the rinsed saucepan. Meanwhile, vigorously whisk the blood into the soup, whisking continuously. The soup separates easily. Take the pan off the heat, add the spices, wine and fruit stock. Taste and adjust seasoning. Keep the soup warm in a bain marie so that it doesn't separate.

Serve the soup as hot as possible with the giblets, fruit and sliced goose liver sausage arranged on a platter.

There are two alternatives to this. One is a Polish blood soup called Tchernina. The other is to make a traditional Chinese hot and sour soup. This has ox's blood drizzled into it as a finishing touch. The important thing is that the soup is hot enough for the blood to thicken in it, rather like adding a raw egg to French onion soup.

For the main course we recommend jugged hare and blood sausages - together if you wish to make a sensation, separately for a more subtle, calculated effect.

JUGGED HARE

There are those who believe that jugged hare can be made without the blood, that it tastes just as good using stock instead. One should treat such persons with contempt. They are the sort who think that the Brahms double concerto sounds just as good without the cello part.

SADDLE OF HARE

$^1/_2$ LB PIECE OF FAT BACON

2 LARGE ONIONS

4 - 5 CARROTS

BOUQUET GARNI

PINCH OF MACE

6 CLOVES

12 PEPPERCORNS

1 TEASPOON OF SALT

1 GLASS OF PORT

$^1/_4$ PT OF RED WINE

1 TABLESPOON OF REDCURRANT JELLY

Don't forget to ask the butcher for the blood. Chop the meat into 11/2 inch pieces. Separate the legs from the thighs. Fry the bacon for 3 to 4 minutes in a large pan. Add the meat, vegetables and brown as evenly as possible. Put into a casserole with herbs, mace, cloves, salt and peppercorns. Cover tightly with foil and then the lid. Stand in boiling water (this is why it is 'jugged' hare) which comes at least half-way up the pot. Keep the vessel covered so the water does not boil off. Boil for three hours, restoring the level of water if necessary.

After three hours, lift the lid of the pot containing the hare and add red wine, port and redcurrant jelly. Add a little salt and pepper. Add the blood of the hare and stir in well. The dish can be reheated a little, but on no account allow it to boil, otherwise the blood will curdle.

Jugged hare is very rich and is best served with something plain. Hungarian blood fritters, for instance. These might be served in homage to Countess Elisabeth.

BLOOD FRITTERS

BLOOD OF 1 GOOSE OR DUCK, OR 1 PT OF PIG'S BLOOD

SALT

2 OZ FAT

1 LARGE ONION

PAPRIKA

Slice the onion and lightly fry in the fat. Slice or cube the congealed blood and add it to the onion. Season it with salt and paprika. Fry for 6 to 8 minutes, stirring continuously. Serve with boiled potatoes which have been tossed in hot bacon dripping, and accompany with a salad such as cucumber.

BLOOD SAUSAGES
(1) - BOUDIN NOIR

400G ONIONS, CHOPPED

100G LARD

750G FRESH PORK FAT, DICED

BOUQUET GARNI

40G SALT

1 GLASS WHITE WINE

$^1/_2$ TSP BLACK PEPPER

$^1/_2$ TSP ALLSPICE

$^3/_4$ CUP CREAM

HOG CASINGS

Fry the onions in the lard until soft. Soften the pork fat to the point of translucency by heating gently in a pan. Tip in the onions and bouquet garni and cook for 20 minutes. Take the pan off the heat and stir continuously as you pour in the blood. 1 litre of pig's blood, which you prevent from coagulating either by draining it straight from the hanging carcass and stirring over hot embers, or by diluting with 1 tablespoon of wine vinegar. Add wine, salt, pepper and allspice. Sieve out any unmelted fat, add cream and stir thoroughly. Pour the mixture through a funnel into the casing which you have taken the precaution of knotting at one end (or wear stout galoshes). Squeeze it along with your hand until you have 4 to 6 inches of filled sausage, then twist repeatedly and carry on filling to form into links. Knot the top end and drop into boiling water. Cook the *boudins* at just below boiling point for 20 minutes and prick as they swim to the surface. When a brown liquid oozes out they're done. Drain and cool.

To serve, grill for 5 minutes on each side and lay on apples fried in pork fat. Alternatively, fry onions in pork fat, keep them warm while you fry the *boudin* in the same fat, then serve together with pieces of pig's liver and heart. This, says Elizabeth David, is a good, rough, old-fashioned French way of serving the blood sausage, 'but is not exactly easy on the digestion.' Well worth trying.

Two pretty variations from Alsace: *Schwarzwurst* (black sausage) - made from pig's blood, crackling, ears, boned head and trotters, fat and onions - and *Zungenwurst* (tongue sausage) - which is a normal *boudin noir* ornamented with geometrically inserted pieces of pig's tongue wrapped in bacon.

BLOOD SAUSAGES
(2) - GOGUES

These are from Anjou, and are less crude than their colleagues, as the presence of cream and vegetables suggests.

9 OZ EACH OF SPINACH BEET, SPINACH,

LETTUCE AND ONIONS

SALT

PEPPER

3 TABLESPOONS LARD

9 OZ STREAKY BACON

CINNAMON

MIXED SPICE

6 TABLESPOONS DOUBLE CREAM

$^1/_2$ PINT PIG'S BLOOD

HOG CASING

Chop the vegetables, add salt and pepper, set aside for 12 hours. Dice the bacon and fry without browning. Melt the lard in a casserole, gently cook the vegetables in it, then add the bacon together with a dash of cinnamon and mixed spice. Stir. Remove from heat. Add cream and blood. Fill the hog casing, and make a twist every 6 inches. Tie the open end and poach in hot (not quite boiling) water for half an hour. Prick the skins as the sausages float to the surface. Drain and cool. Slice thickly and fry in butter or lard until they turn brown.

Blood sausages
(3) - Welsh Blood Pudding

———•◦•———

This refreshing recipe comes from the Principality via Antony and Araminta Hippisley Coxe, authors of *The Book of Sausages*.

THE BLOOD OF A FRESHLY KILLED PIG

1 PINT WELL WATER

SALT AND PEPPER

ONIONS

HERBS TO TASTE

A LITTLE FAT FROM THE INTESTINE

OATMEAL

HOG CASINGS

Gather the blood into a big bowl while it is still warm and stir until it is cold. Add the well water and a little salt and leave the liquid to stand overnight. Wash the casing well and also leave to stand overnight in salt water.

Next day, chop the onions and the fat and coat them with oatmeal, season with herbs and pepper and stir into the blood. Push the mixture into the casing. Tie both ends with string; boil for about 30 minutes and then hang to dry. It can be served sliced and fried with rashers of thick, salty bacon.

———•◦•———

Finding a dessert to round off this meal is not easy. Robert May in his book *Accomplisht Cook*, written in 1660, mentions a very fine fancy. A stag is sculpted out of painted sugar and almond paste and filled with softly set claret jelly. The stag is then stuck with an arrow in such a way that when it is drawn by one of the guests, the jelly pours out like blood oozing from a wound. An amusing alternative to the stag would be a Saint Sebastian, life-size perhaps, thus allowing more than one guest the pleasure of drawing an arrow. For those who may not have the time to sculpt a life-size St. Sebastian, the following Scottish recipe is a possibility.

$^1/_2$ PT OF BLOOD

$^1/_2$ PT OF CREAM

SALT

CINNAMON

NUTMEG

A SPRIG OF MINT

CHIVES

FAT

Lamb's blood is recommended as being the sweetest. Stir it and remove any clot, or else pass it through a sieve. Mix it together with the cream. Season with the salt, a pinch of cinnamon and a pinch of nutmeg. Finely chop a sprig of mint and the chives. Mince the fat and add it with the mint and chives to the mixture. Pour into a heavy saucepan and cook in the oven or on top of the stove.

If that doesn't appeal as a dessert, try this instead. It's a traditional recipe at Boodle's, with a difference - rather than using ordinary oranges, use blood oranges.

CRIMSON TART

4 BLOOD ORANGES

2 LEMONS

$1^1/_2$ PINTS OF CREAM

8 SPONGE CAKES

$^1/_4$ LB CASTER SUGAR

Mix the juice of all the fruit with the grated rind of a lemon and 2 oranges. Stir in the sugar, and beat in one pint of the cream. Blend well. Cut each sponge cake into four pieces and put into a bowl. Pour the mixture over the cakes. Chill for several hours and pour the remaining whipped cream on top before serving.

A daring alternative is Blutwurst. These are eaten cold in Germany. Their purplish-crimson flesh is highly suited to the Decadent table, and their cloying, fungal, slightly rotten taste makes them a lavish and unsettling dessert.

BLUTWURST

DICED BACON

CALF'S OR PIG'S LUNG

PIG'S BLOOD

CLOVES, MACE, MARJORAM

BULLOCK RUNNERS, CUT TO 15 INCH LENGTHS

Season the blood with the herbs and spices in a bowl. Boil the chopped lungs and bacon. Tie one end of the bullock runner with string, fill with blood, lungs and bacon, tie the other end, and boil for half an hour. Serve cold in very thin slices, with a blanket of chocolate sauce.

As for drink to accompany this meal, the most obvious choice is Egri Bikavér, the famous Hungarian red wine otherwise known as "Bulls' Blood". There is a legend that during the Middle Ages bulls' blood was indeed added to the wine to give it its dark red, almost black colour. The other possibilities are somewhat more recherché. At certain high-class Japanese restaurants one can sample a mixture of sake and turtle's blood, while the equivalent establishment in the Philippines offers fortifying draughts of snake blood, poured straight from the serpent's throat freshly slit at the customer's table.

The Glass of Blood

by Jean Lorrain

She stands at a window beside a lilac curtain patterned with silver thistle. She is supporting herself upon the sill while looking out over the courtyard of the hotel, at the avenue lined with chestnut-trees, resplendent in their green autumn foliage. Her pose is business-like, but just a little theatrical: her face uplifted, her right arm carelessly dangling.

Behind her, the high wall of the vast hallway curves away into the distance; beneath her feet the polished parquet floor carries the reflected gleam of the early morning sun. On the opposite wall is a mirror which reflects the sumptuous and glacially pure interior, which is devoid of furniture and ornament save for a large wooden table with curved legs. On top of the table is an immense vase of Venetian glass, moulded in the shape of a conch-shell lightly patterned with flecks of gold; and in the vase is a sheaf of delicate flowers.

All the flowers are white: white irises, white tulips, white narcissi. Only the textures are different, some as glossy as pearls, others sparkling like frost, others as smooth as drifting snow; the petals seem as delicate as translucent porcelain, glazed with a chimerical beauty. The only hint of colour is the pale gold at the heart of each narcissus. The scent which the flowers exude is strangely ambivalent: ethereal, but with a certain sharpness somehow suggestive of cruelty, whose hardness threatens to transform the irises into iron pikes, the tulips into jagged-edged cups, the narcissi into shooting-stars fallen from the winter sky.

And the woman, whose shadow extends from where she stands at the window to the foot of the table - she too has something of that same ambivalent coldness and apparent cruelty. She is dressed as if to resemble the floral spray, in a long dress of white velvet trimmed with fine-spun lace; her gold-filigreed belt has slipped down to rest upon her hips. Her pale-skinned arms protrude from loose satin sleeves and the white nape of her neck is visible beneath her ash-blonde hair. Her profile is clean-cut; her eyes are steel-grey; her pallid face seems bloodless save for the faint pinkness of her thin, half-smiling lips. The overall effect is that the woman fits her surroundings perfectly; she is clearly from the north - a typical woman of the fair-skinned kind, cold and refined but possessed of a controlled and meditative passion.

She is slightly nervous, occasionally glancing away from the window into the room; when she does so her eyes cannot help but encounter her image reflected in the mirror on the opposite wall. When that happens, she laughs; the sight reminds her of Juliet awaiting Romeo - the costume is almost right, and the pose is perfect.

Come, night! come Romeo! come, thou day in night!
For thou wilt lie upon the wings of night
Whiter than new snow upon a raven's back.

As she looks into the mirror she sees herself once again in the long white robe of the daughter of the Capulets; she strikes the remembered pose, and stands no longer in the plush corridor of the hotel but upon a balcony mounted above the wings of the stage in a great theatre, beneath the dazzling glare of the electric lights, before a Verona of painted cloth, tormenting herself with whispered words of love.

Wilt thou be gone? it is not yet near day:
It was the nightingale, and not the lark,
That pierced the fearful hollow of thine ear.
Nightly she sings on yon pomegranate-tree:
Believe me, love, it was the nightingale.

And afterwards, how fervently she and her Romeo would be applauded, as they took their bows before the house!

After the triumph of Juliet, there had been the triumph of Marguerite, then the triumph of Ophelia - the Ophelia which she had recreated for herself, her unforgettable performance now enshrined in legend: *That's rosemary, that's for remembrance; pray you, love, remember!* All dressed in white, garlanded with flowers in the birch-wood! Then she had played the Queen of the Night in *The Magic Flute*; and Flotow's *Martha*; the fiancée of *Tannhauser*; Elsa in *Lohengrin*. She had played the parts of all the great heroines, personifying them as blondes, bringing them to life with the crystal clarity of her soprano voice and the perfection of her virginal profile, haloed by her golden hair.

She had made Juliet blonde, and Rosalind, and Desdemona, so that Paris, St. Petersburg, Vienna and London had not only accepted blondes in those roles but had applauded blondes - and had come, in the end, to expect and demand blondes. That was all her doing: the triumph of La Barnarina, who, as a little girl, had run bare-legged across the steppe, asking no more and no less than any other girl of her age, lying in wait for the sleighs and the troikas which passed through the tiny village - a poor hamlet of less than a hundred souls, with thirty muzhik peasants and a priest.

She was the daughter of peasants, but today she is a marquise - an authentic marquise, a millionaire four times over, the wedded wife of an ambassador whose name is inscribed in the *livre d'or* of the Venetian nobles, and entered upon the fortieth page of the Almanack of Gotha.

But this is still the same girl who once lived in the steppes, wild and indomitable. Even when she ceased to play in the falling snow, the snow continued to fall within her soul. She never sought lovers among the wealthy men and the crowned princes who prostrated themselves before her; her heart, like her voice, remained faultless. The reputation, temperament and talent of the woman partook of exactly the same crystalline transparency and icy clarity.

She is married now, though it is a marriage which was not contracted out of love, nor in the cause of ambition. She has enriched her husband more than he has enriched her, and she cares nothing for the fact that he was once a celebrity of the Tuileries in the days of the Empire, or that he became a star of the season at Biarritz as soon as he returned to Paris from the Italian court, following the disaster of Sedan.

Why, then, did she marry that one rather than another?

In fact, it was because she fell in love with his daughter.

The man was a widower, a widower with a very charming child, just fourteen years old. The daughter, Rosaria, was an Italian from Madrid - her mother had been Spanish - with a face like a Murillo archangel: huge dark eyes, moist and radiant, and a wide, laughing mouth. She had all the childish, yet instinctively amorous, gaiety of the most favoured children of the sunny

Mediterranean.

Badly brought up by the widower whom she adored, and spoiled by that overgenerous treatment which is reserved for the daughters of the nobility, this child had been seized by an adoring passion for the diva whom she had so often applauded in the theatre. Because she was endowed with a tolerably pleasant voice the child had come to cherish the dream of taking lessons from La Barnarina. That dream, as soon as it was once denied, had quickly become an overpowering desire: an obsession, an *idée fixe*; and the marquis had been forced to give way. One day he had brought his daughter to the singer's home, secure in the knowledge that she would be politely received - La Barnarina was accepted as an equal by members of the finest aristocracies in Europe - but fully expecting her request to be refused. But the child, with all the gentleness of a little girl, with the half-grandiose manners of the young aristocrat, with the innocent warmth of the novice in matters of love, had amused, seduced and conquered the diva.

Rosaria had become her pupil.

In time, she had come to regard her almost as a daughter.

Ten months after that first presentation, however, the marquis had been recalled by his government to Milan, where he expected to be asked to accept a position as envoy to some remote region - either Smyrna or Constantinople. He intended, of course, to take his daughter with him.

La Barnarina had not anticipated any such event, and had been unable to foresee what effect it would have on her.

When the time for the little girl's departure came, La Barnarina had felt a sudden coldness possessing her heart, and suddenly knew that the separation would be intolerable: this child had become part of her, her own soul and her own flesh. La Barnarina, the cold and the dispassionate, had found the rock upon which her wave must break; the claims of love which she had kept at bay for so long now exerted themselves with a vengeance.

La Barnarina was a mother who had never given birth, as immaculate as the divine mothers of the Eastern religions. In the flesh which had never yearned to produce fruit of its own there had been lit a very ardent passion for the child of another's loins.

Rosaria had also been reduced to tears by the thought of

the parting; and the marquis soon became annoyed by the way the two women persistently sobbed in one another's arms. He quickly lost patience with the business of trying to patch up the situation, but hesitated to suggest the only possible solution.

"Oh papa, what are we to do?" pleaded Rosaria, in a choked whisper.

"Yes, marquis, tell us what to do," added the singer, as she stood before him embracing the young girl.

So the marquis, spreading his arms wide with the palms open, smiling as sadly as Cassandra, was left to point the way to the obvious conclusion.

"I believe, my dear children, there is one way..."

And with a grand salute, a truly courtly gesture, to the unhappy actress, he said:

"You must leave the stage and become my wife, so that you may take charge of the child!"

And so she married him, leaving behind the former life which she had loved so ardently and which had made her so rich. At the height of her career, and with her talent still in full bloom, she had left behind the Opera, her public, and all her triumphs. The star became a marquise - all for the love of Rosaria.

It is that same Rosaria for whom she is waiting at this very moment, slightly ruffled by impatience, as she stands before the high window in her white lace and her soft white velvet, in her pose which is just a little theatrical because she cannot help remembering Juliet awaiting the arrival of Romeo!

Romeo! As she silently stammers the name of Romeo, La Barnarina becomes even paler.

In Shakespeare's play, as she knows only too well, Romeo dies and Juliet cannot survive without his love; the two of them yield up their souls together, the one upon the corpse of the other - a dark wedding amid the shadows of the tomb. La Barnarina - who is, after all, the daughter of Russian peasants - is superstitious, and cannot help but regret her involuntary reverie.

Here, of all places, and now, of all times, she has dreamed of Romeo!

The reason for her distress is that Rosaria, alas, has come to know suffering. Since the departure of her father she has changed, and changed considerably. The poor darling's features have been transfigured: the lips which were so red are now tinged with violet; dark shadowy circles like blurred splashes of kohl are visible beneath her eyes and they continue to deepen; she has lost that faint ambience, reminiscent of fresh raspberries, which testifies to the health of adolescents. She has never complained, never having been one to seek sympathy, but it did not take long for La Barnarina to become alarmed once she saw that the girl's complexion had taken on the pallor of wax, save for feverish periods when it would be inflamed by the colour of little red apples.

"It is nothing, my dear!" the child said, so lovingly - but La Barnarina hurried to seek advice.

The results of her consultations had been quite explicit, and La Barnarina felt that she had been touched by Death's cold hand. "You love that girl too much, madame," they had said, "and the child in her turn has learned to love you too much; you are killing her with your caresses."

Rosaria did not understand, but her mother understood only too well; from that day on she had begun to cut the child off from her kisses and embraces; desperately, she had gone from doctor to doctor - seeking out the celebrated and the obscure, the empirically-inclined and the homeopathic - but at every turn she had been met with a sad shake of the head. Only one of them had taken it upon himself to indicate a possible remedy: Rosaria must join the ranks of the consumptives who go at dawn to the abattoirs to drink lukewarm blood freshly taken from the calves which are bled to make veal.

On the first few occasions, the marquise had taken it upon herself to lead the child down into the abattoirs; but the horrid odour of the blood, the warm carcasses, the bellowing of the beasts as they came to be slaughtered, the carnage of the butchering...all that had caused her terrible anguish, and had sickened her heart. She could not stand it.

Rosaria had been less intimidated. She had bravely swallowed the lukewarm blood, saying only: "This red milk is a little thick for my taste."

Now, it is a governess who has the task of conducting the

girl into the depths; every morning they go down, at five or six o'clock, to that devils' kitchen beneath the rue de Flandre, to an enclosure where the blood is drained from the living calves, to make the white and tender meat.

And while the young girl makes her descent into that place, where bright- burning fires warm the water in porcelain bathtubs to scald the flesh of the slaughtered beasts, La Barnarina stays here, by the window in the great hallway, perfectly tragic in her velvet and her lace, mirroring in her mode of dress the snow-whiteness of the narcissi, the frost-whiteness of the tulips, and the nacreous whiteness of the irises; here, striking a pose with just a hint of theatricality, she watches.

She keeps watch upon the courtyard of the hotel, and the empty avenue beyond the gate, and her anguish reaches into the uttermost depths of her soul while she anticipates the first kiss which the child will place upon her lips, as soon as she returns: a kiss which always carries an insipid trace of the taste of blood and a faint hint of that odour which perpetually defiles the rue de Flandre, but which, strangely enough, she does not detest at all - quite the contrary - when it is upon the warm lips of her beloved Rosaria.

The Glass of Blood by Jean Lorrain translated by Brian Stableford is published in *The Dedalus Book of Decadence (Moral Ruins)* edited by Brian Stableford (1990).

CHAPTER 6

CORRUPTION AND DECAY

One of Durian Gray's favourite books, and one to which he returned time and again, was T.M. Heathcote's *The Lives of the Dandies*. Not only was it an inexhaustible source of ideas about decor, costume and manners, but it had the ability to lift Durian's spirits when he was feeling maudlin. A character he particularly admired was Sir George Margelle. The following passage describes Heathcote's first meeting with the old man.

————•◦•————

'Whenever I hear mention of Sir George Margelle, I am invariably reminded of a particular quotation from *Hamlet* .

"… to live in the rank sweat of an enseamed bed, stew'd in corruption, honeying and making love over the nasty sty."

These lines epitomise the state into which Sir George had sunk in his old age after a lifetime of dissipation. I remember particularly vividly the first visit I made to his Palladian house in Sussex. I arrived on a bitterly cold day in the winter of 1874. The door was opened to me by a small oleaginous man with sharp features and a disarming smile. He neither looked nor acted like a domestic servant, and I later discovered that he was Sir George's chef and comprised the entire staff, being the only one who was prepared to still tolerate the old roué's behaviour. He showed me through the house and into a study. On entering the room, the first thing I noticed was the sickly sweet smell of flowers which hung heavy on the air. Next to the fireplace, on an elegant daybed lay the enormously corpulent old gentleman. Debauchery had exacted its toll. His body was bloated, his cheeks and eyes blood-shot, and his voice was reduced to a gruff, throaty whisper.

We engaged in conversation for some time. It ranged over several topics, but there was one to which Sir George returned again and again - corruption. I knew that the putrid, the rotten, the diseased, the moribund, the decayed, the cankered, the mouldering had always held a certain fascination for him. Now in his dotage, he had became quite morbidly enthusiastic about this subject. At one point in our conversation he held toward me a copy of the poetry of Charles Baudelaire and asked me to read one of his best-loved poems, entitled *Une Charogne*.

> *Rappelez-vous l'objet que nous vîmes, mon âme,*
> *Ce beau matin d'été si doux:*
> *Au détour d'un sentier une charogne infame*
> *Sur un lit semé de cailloux,*
>
> *Les jambes en l'air, comme une femme lubrique,*
> *Brûlante et suant les poisons,*
> *Ouvrait d'une façon nonchalante et cynique*
> *Son ventre plein d'exhalaisons.*
>
> *Le soleil rayonnait sur cette pourriture,*
> *Comme afin de la cuire à point,*
> *Et de rendre au centuple à la grande Nature*
> *Tout ce qu'ensemble elle avait joint;*
>
> *Et le ciel regardait la carcasse superbe*
> *Comme une fleur s'épanouir.*
> *La puanteur était si forte, que sur l'herbe*
> *Vous crûtes vous évanouir.*
>
> *Les mouches bourdonnaient sur ce ventre putride*
> *D'où sortaient de noirs bataillons*
> *De larves, qui coulaient comme un épais liquide*
> *Le long de ces vivants haillons.*

(Do you remember, my love, the object we saw on that wonderful, calm summer morning. Just off the path lay a vile corpse on a bed of pebbles. It had its legs in the air like a slut. It was smouldering and sweating out poisons. Its fume-filled belly was opened up in a brazen, shameless manner. The sun beat down on this rotting meat, as if to cook it just right, and to give back to great Nature a hundredfold what she had joined together. The sky looked down on this proud carcass which was opening out like a flower. The stench was so strong that you thought you were going to faint. The flies buzzed around its putrid guts from which streamed battalions of black larvae, like thick liquid pouring over these living rags.)

The poem continues in this vein until the end where it becomes a sort of Memento mori. The poet reminds his love that she too will one day be in this state.

> - Et pourtant vous serez semblable à cette ordure,
>   A cette horrible infection,
> Etoile de mes yeux, soleil de ma nature,
>   Vous, mon ange et ma passion.
> Oui! telle vous serez, ô la reine des grâces,
>   Après les derniers sacrements,
> Quand vous irez, sous l'herbe et les floraisons grasses
>   Moisir parmi les ossements.
>
> Alors, ô ma beauté! dites à la vermine
>   Qui vous mangera de baisers,
> Que j'ai gardé la forme et l'essence divine
>   De mes amours décomposés!

(And yet, you, Star of my Eyes, Sun of my Nature, my Angel and my Passion, you will come to resemble this obscenity, this horrible infection. Yes, this is how you will end up, O Queen of the Graces, after the last rites, when you will lie under the grass and the thickly-growing flowers, mouldering among the bones. So, my Beauty, tell the worms as they eat you with their kisses, that I have retained the form and divine essence of our decomposed love.)

I must admit I found the subject matter rather disturbing, but Sir George was obviously delighted with the reading. He sank back in his pillows with a sigh of almost voluptuous contentment. Then he suggested that I might like to stay for a little lunch. I accepted readily, curious to see what sort of regime the old debauchee followed. What I did not realise was that Sir George's predilection for the corrupt and the rotten extended to the food he ate.

We were crossing the domed entrance hall, when the chef appeared with two woodcock and a pheasant. Judging by the smell of them, they had been hanging for some time. The flesh of the fowls' breast appeared dark green in colour. Sir George held the carcasses to his nose, inhaled deeply and told the chef that they were not quite ready. He had noticed the way in which I had recoiled from the birds when they were brought close, however, and as we continued our slow progress towards the dining room, he began a short disquisition, citing Monsieur Brillat-Savarin as his authority, on the optimum condition for cooking and eating pheasant. If it is eaten within three days of its being killed not only does the meat tend to be tough, but its flavour is unremarkable. It lacks the delicacy of fowl and the fragrance of quail, Sir George explained. If, on the other hand, it is left hanging long enough and cooked at just the right moment, its flesh is tender and the taste sublime. It shares the flavour of both poultry and venison. Sir George went on:

" This desirable state is reached only when the bird begins to decompose. Only then does the flesh begin to loosen and the fragrance develop."

In Sir George's opinion, the bird should be in such a state of putrefaction that when it is spit roasted one has to wrap a slice of bread around it and tie it up with string to prevent it falling apart. I informed Sir George that I had never been able to eat pheasant after the death of a favourite great uncle of mine who had eaten the bird in such numbers that he had succumbed to lead poisoning as a result of the quantity of shot that he consumed along with them. I was delighted to hear that we would not be eating the pheasant, but immediately became anxious as to what exactly would be served.

We sat at either end of a mahogany table, in a small, heavily mirrored dining room. At Sir George's right elbow stood a large earthenware jar. He removed the lid and took out what appeared to be a lump of grey, dried mud. " Thousand Year Old Eggs," I was informed. " From China, dear boy."

Once the mud and the shell had been carefully removed, Sir George sliced the egg into quarters. It was a greenish-yellow in colour and had a pungent, cheesy smell to it. As I was contemplating the prospect of having actually to swallow one of these, Sir George called in the chef to give a detailed account of how the eggs were prepared. The fact that they were only several months old did nothing to restore my rapidly dwindling appetite and I viewed the arrival of the second course with trepidation.

The chef re-appeared eventually with a large dish of meat and vegetables which looked remarkably appetising. I asked him whether this dish had any particular name. " Olla podrida," he replied. This left me none the wiser. I glanced in the direction of my host who looked up from his plate and informed me that it was Spanish for 'rotten stew'.

Aren't all Spanish stews rotten, I thought.

As with the first course, Sir George called upon his chef to recite to us the way in which he had prepared this dish. He read out the recipe he had followed from a book by Mr Richard Ford entitled *Gatherings from Spain* which was published some thirty years ago.

It was a very strange affair. There was my host, bent over his plate, and I, sitting somewhat rigidly, eating in silence while the chef intoned this recipe in much the same way that a monk might read from holy scripture while the brothers eat their midday meal in the refectory. It seemed that Sir George took in the reading with as much relish as he took in his rotten stew. The reading ended, I remember, with the following panegyric:

" No violets come up to the perfume which a cooking *olla* casts before it; the mouth watering bystanders sigh, as they see and smell the rich freight steaming away from them."

A similar scene took place when a rook pie was presented. I declined this dish, saying that I was already satisfied, although in fact I have an aversion to carrion. For Sir George on the other hand, this was precisely what most appealed to him. Again we sat and listened to the chef explain how he had prepared the pie. At one point, Sir George interrupted briefly to inform me about a

Medieval Arabic recipe he had recently come across which produced condiments from rotted barley dough. As the chef continued the explanation of his method, Sir George spooned quantities of gooseberry jelly on to his plate. He wore an expression on his face which could only be described as lascivious.

After the rook pie, we were offered a selection of cheeses, each in an advanced state of decay. I again declined, despite feeling increasing pangs of hunger. Sir George helped himself to those cheeses which displayed the highest proportion of mould.

We came finally to the dessert. My host leant forward and informed me in that hoarse, slurred whisper that this was his favourite course. It came as no surprise to me when the chef entered with a bowl of medlars - like the pheasant, medlars, which resemble grenadillas, are best eaten when they have begun to decompose. To accompany the medlars was a bowl of 'pire fotute', a precise translation of which need not concern us here. This, my host informed me, was a Sicilian dish made from rotting pears which tasted like chocolate. I took his word for it. Along with the fruit we drank a glass of Sauternes. Needless to say, Sir George waxed lyrical on the subject of 'la pourriture noble' or noble rot. He gave a most painterly description of the grey-green mould which is allowed to cover the Sauternes grapes before they are picked and which imparts that characteristic sweetness to the wine. The unsteadiness of his hand meant that a large proportion of the contents of his glass dribbled out of the side of his mouth or down his chin.

Just when I thought the meal had reached its conclusion, a large porcelain jar with a closely fitting lid was borne in ceremoniously. For one ghastly moment I thought Sir George was about to recommence the meal with his ancient Chinese eggs. What lay in store was something much worse. As my host was prising the lid off the jar, he told me that it contained a fruit - the durian - whose flavour was second to none, and quite unlike anything I had ever tasted before. Unfortunately I never did taste this extraordinary fruit. I never got beyond the smell. When the lid was finally removed from the jar, the stench that filled the room was indescribable. The ony thing I might compare it to is the sweet smell of rotting flesh. I hurriedly excused myself and left the room.

As I made my way back to London later that afternoon, it occurred to me that despite the old man's morbid fascination with decay and corruption, he ate extremely well. I, however, was looking forward to the piece of fresh fish my housekeeper had promised me.'

RICHARD FORD'S
OLLA PODRIDA

Having specified the need for two earthenware pots on the stove each boiling separately, Mr Ford continues:

" Place into No.1 garbanzos (chick peas) which have been placed to soak overnight, add a good piece of beef, a chicken, a large piece of bacon. Let it boil once quickly then let it simmer; it requires four or five hours to be well done. Meanwhile, place into no 2, with water, whatever vegetables are to be had, lettuces, cabbage, a slice of gourd, of beef, carrots, beans, celery, endive, onions and garlic, long peppers. These must be previously well washed and cut, as if they were destined to make a salad; then add red sausages, or chorizos, half a salted pig's face which should have been soaked overnight. When all is sufficiently boiled, strain off the water and throw it away. Remember constantly to skim the scum off both saucepans. When all this is sufficiently dressed, take a large dish, lay in the bottom the vegetables, the beef in the centre, flanked by the bacon, chicken and pig's face. The sausages should be arranged around, en couronne; pour over some of the soup of No.1 and serve hot."

ROOK PIE

Soak the legs and breasts of six young rooks in salt water overnight. Drain them and place in a pie dish, adding a few pieces of fat bacon cut into chunks. The meat is then covered with stock and seasoned with salt and pepper.

For the pastry, take 1lb flour, cut and rub in $^1/_2$ lb of fat, add pepper and salt to season, followed by 4 ounces each of currants and stoned raisins. Add sufficient water to make a stiff paste and turn on to a floured board. Roll out to about 3/4 inch thick and place on top of the pie dish. Cover the pie with greaseproof paper and tie it down in a pudding cloth. Place this in a large pan of boiling water and cook it for three hours.

CHAPTER 7

I CAN RECOMMEND
THE POODLE

Strolling through the gardens of the Palais Royal in Paris, sometime in the 1850s, one would no doubt have come across a number of heart-warming sights - a paterfamilias in a black frock coat sits on a bench watching his three pretty children playing with the kitten he has just given them. A young lady, dressed expensively and impractically in white, bends to pick up her yorkshire terrier and adjust the bow on the top of its head. And amid these scenes of bourgeois rectitude one might well have caught a glimpse of the extravagant figure of poet and novelist, Gérard de Nerval. He was unmistakable, less for himself though than for his little pet, which he dragged along at the end of a length of pale blue ribbon. Literally 'dragged', because his little pet was a lobster.

De Nerval had close links with the Decadent movement. His writings, much admired by Baudelaire and Gautier, were often the product of bizarre imaginings and exotic situations. However, poor Gérard spent most of his working life engaged in an unequal struggle against poverty and madness. He finally brought it all to an untimely close at the end of a rope, dangling from a lamp post in the rue de la Vieille Lanterne. History does not record what happened to his pet, but no doubt at some point it was plunged live into a pot of boiling water and eaten.

Of course, had one wandered up to any other pet owners in the gardens of the Palais Royal at that time and suggested, for example, that the Mademoiselle's adorable little terrier or the sweet fluffy kitten that Monsieur's children are playing with so gaily might be as tasty as de Nerval's pet, these suggestions would have been greeted with the utmost horror. Accusations of Monster! Degenerate! Ogre! and the like, would have rained down on one's head.

Interestingly, however, no more than a decade and a half after the death of de Nerval, two cookbooks were published in Paris which contained recipes not only for the preparation and cooking of dog, but of cat as well. Indeed, according to Henry Labouchère, who was staying in the French capital during the autumn and winter of 1870, dishes of cat, dog and rat had begun to appear quite regularly in Parisian restaurants. The following are some of the observations he recorded on this matter:

Cats have risen in the market - a good fat one now costs 20 francs. Those that remain are exceedingly wild.

This morning I had a salmis of rats - it was excellent - something between frog and rabbit. I breakfasted with the correspondents of two of your contemporaries. One of them after a certain amount of hesitation allowed me to help him to a leg of rat; after eating it he was as anxious as a terrier for more. The other, however, scornfully refused to share in the repast. As he got through his potion of salted horse which rejoiced in the name of beef, he regarded us with horror and disgust. I remember when I was in Egypt that my feelings towards the natives were of a similar nature when I saw them eating rat. The older one grows, the more tolerant one becomes. If ever I am again in Africa I shall eat the national dish whenever I get the chance. I was curious to see whether the proprietor of the restaurant would boldly call rat, rat on my bill. His heart failed him - it figures as a salmi of game.

All the animals in the zoological gardens have been killed except the monkeys; they are kept alive from a vague and Darwinian notion that they are our relatives, or at least relatives of some of the members of the government, to whom, in the matter of beauty, nature has not been bountiful.

In the rue Blanche, there is a butcher who sells dogs, rats and cats. He has many customers, but it is amusing to see them sneak into the shop after carefully looking around to make sure none of their acquaintances is near. A prejudice has arisen against rats because the doctors say that their flesh is full of trichinae. I own for my part I have a gulity feeling when I eat dog, the friend of man. I had a slice of spaniel the other day - it was by no means bad, something like lamb, but I felt like a cannibal. Epicures in dog flesh tell me that poodle is by far the best, and recommended me to avoid bulldog, which is coarse and tasteless. I really think that dogs have some means of communicating with each other and have discovered that their old friends want to devour them. The humblest of street curs growls when anyone looks at them. Figaro has a story that a man was followed for a mile by a party of dogs barking fiercely at his heels. He could not understand to what their attentions were due until he remembered that he had eaten a rat for breakfast. The friend of another journalist who ate a dog called Fox, says that whenever anyone calls out 'Fox' he feels an irresistible impulse which forces him to jump up.

Cat, dog, rat and horse are all very well as novelties, but taken habitually they do not assimilate with my inner man. Horse, doctors say, is heating: I only wish it would heat me.

Now, it is perhaps only fair to point out that Henry Labouchère, despite his very gallic sounding name, was in fact an Englishman, and a journalist, and his observations of daily life in the French capital were made at a time when it was being besieged by the Prussian army. And, admittedly, by January 1871 the Prussians had succeeded in starving the citizens of Paris into surrender. So it is not altogether surprising that there was such a trade in the sort of creatures which did not normally grace the tables of the Parisian bourgeoisie. However, given that the flavour of dog is strong but not disagreeable and is comparable to mutton, venison or goat, the question remains as to why this taboo is still so firmly in place?

At this point, Mademoiselle would no doubt scoop her little darling protectively into her arms and state that the consumption of dog is the practice only of barbarous peoples.

Like the ancient Greeks, for example? This is how Porphyrus, the third century Greek writer, explains the origins of eating dog:

'One day, a dog was being offered in sacrifice at a temple. When a piece of the victim fell to the floor, the priest picked it up in order to replace it on the altar. However, the meat was very hot and the priest burnt his fingers. Naturally, without thinking, he put his fingers to his mouth and found that the juices on them tasted good. After the ceremony was over, he ate half the dog and took the other half home to his wife. From then on,

after each sacrifice, the priest and his wife feasted on the victim. Word of this soon spread all over town; everybody tasted it and in a very short while roast dog was to be found at all the best tables. To begin with, people used puppies in their cooking as their meat was naturally more tender; later, when there was a shortage of these, larger dogs were used.'

Or perhaps Mademoiselle was referring to the 'barbarous Chinese'? The Han dynasty (202 B.C. to 221 A.D.), perhaps the greatest of the Chinese dynasties, saw the appearance of a book of ritual, known as the *Li-chi*. The *Li-chi* contained eight delicacies which could be prepared for the elderly on ceremonial occasions. One of the recipes cited involves taking the liver of a dog and coating it in a thin layer of its own fat. The fat-covered liver is then moistened and roasted. At the last moment the liver is removed from the roasting dish and placed directly in the flames. This sears it and produces a crackling effect. It sounds delicious.

Another of the great civilisations, the Aztecs, raised a breed of hairless chihuahuas especially for eating. When the Conquistadors arrived and found dog on the menu, they were of the same opinion as Mademoiselle, that this was evidence of the worst form of barbarism. They, the Spaniards, used dogs as befits civilised and Christian men - to hunt down fugitive Indians and tear them to pieces.

Quite frankly, between the ancient Greeks, the Chinese and the Aztecs, it is difficult to conceive of more noble origins for a particular culinary practice!

Meanwhile, Monsieur, quickly gathering his children and their kitten about him, would argue that however others may behave, we Europeans do not eat dog. They are unclean and are carrion-feeders. Monsieur's argument would cut little ice with the Alpine Swiss who eat dried dog meat and have a recipe called *Gedorrtes hundefleisch*. Or with the people of Vicenza where cat was a standard dish, until the arrival of the supermarket.

No, the truth is that no compelling argument exists as to why dogs, cats or rats should not appear on the menu of a highly esteemed restaurant or on the table at an elegant supper party. It seems much more likely that the problem stems from a lack of good recipes. So here are some suggestions.

As always the success of a dish begins with the quality of the produce. When it comes to choosing your animal, some pointers (no pun intended) have already been provided. I think we can safely accept Labouchère's recommendation of spaniel, although the advice he was given that poodle is superior to bulldog ("coarse and tasteless") may have been prompted by anti-British sentiment. As far as cat is concerned, one simply has to work on the principle of the younger the better. With regard to rat, on the other hand, no lesser an authority than the *Larousse Gastronomique* states quite clearly that the tastiest rats are to be found in wine cellars. Presumably this is based on the notion that if they have been lapping up any spillage from the barrels, they will effectively be marinated from within, although the *Larousse* does not say if one can taste the difference between, say, an Haut Brion rat and a Cos d'Estournel rat.

Of the two following recipes, the second comes from Cameroun and recommends that only castrated male dogs should be consumed. The first is a classic dog dish from the Philippines.

MANILA HOT DOG

Take one 6 - 8lb dog. Chop off head, paws and tail. Paunch and skin it, then bone it. Cut the meat into stew sized chunks. Place in a large deep pan and cover it with water. Bring to the boil and cook for ten minutes. The smell and the flavour can be too strong at this point, in the same way that mature goat is. In this case, parboil the meat again, or even a third time. Place the meat in a large bowl and marinate for at least half an hour. Half a cup of vinegar; 1 bay leaf, 2-3 fresh hot peppers, chopped; 1 onion, chopped; 4-5 cloves of garlic, crushed and chopped; two cups of water, salt to taste. Place meat and marinade in a saucepan, bring to the boil, cover, reduce heat and simmer for 2-3 hours, or until meat is tender. Remove cover from pan and cook further until all the water has evaporated. Have ready some hot chilli sauce and adjust the seasoning with it. Must be very spicy. Serve with rice.

DOG À LA BETI

ONE DOG

SALT

SMALL-LEAVED BASIL

SKIN OF A GARLIC PLANT

PEPPER

'ODJOM'

CITRONELLA

ONIONS

SWEET BANANA ('ODZOE BETI' VARIETY)

BANANA LEAVES

This recipe requires a few preliminaries. Prior to being killed, the dog should be tied to a post for a day and hit with small sticks, to 'shift' the fat in the adipose tissue. After killing, it is cut up into chunks. The skin is scorched over a fire and scraped with a knife. The bowels are emptied, cleaned and rolled up. The pieces of meat are washed and scraped several times until there is no trace of blood or dirt left in the water. The stiff main veins of the banana leaves are skinned, then softened over a fire. The leaves are placed in a criss-cross fashion in a big pan. The pieces of meat are mixed with all the condiments in a separate pan.

This seasoned meat and some sweet bananas of the 'Odzoe beti' variety are placed on the prepared leaves. The leaves are tied together with banana fibre to make a packet. This packet is braised in a pot whose base has been covered with banana leaves. Water is added only up to the mid-point so that it cannot penetrate the packet during the cooking.

Cooking the packet takes eight to nine hours. Once done, the food is served immediately. It is a noble dish reserved for the elders of the village.

The sweet bananas absorb the fat exuded by the chunks of

meat in the course of its cooking. Bananas so prepared are considered succulent.

Cat with polenta is a traditional dish from Alta Brianza. It involved leaving the creature for several days in the snow as a method of tenderising the meat. This following recipe, however, comes from Northern Spain.

CAT IN TOMATO SAUCE

Make a marinade from a cup of vinegar, some sprigs of thyme and two cloves of garlic, finely chopped.

Skin the cat. (Remember, there are more ways than one!) Then gut and wash it well. Cut it into pieces and put them into the marinade in a pot. Leave it overnight.

The following day, add 2 pounds of chopped tomatoes, a tablespoon of ground red pepper, two apples split in half, half a chopped onion and a cup of oil. Bring to the boil, then lower the heat and simmer until the meat is tender. Strain the liquid and then return to the pot. Bring it to the boil for a short while, then serve.

When it comes to rat, one only has to turn to the *Larousse gastronomique* to find the following delicious recipe:

ENTRECOTE À LA BORDELAISE

Skin and de-gut your rat. Rub with a thick sauce of olive oil and crushed shallots. Add salt and pepper. Make a fire from broken wine barrels. Grill the prepared carcass over it. The Larousse recommends that the rat is served with a *Bordelaise* sauce, made according to the recipe of the great French gastronome, Curnonsky. Add six shallots to half a cup of red Bordeaux in a small pan and cook for a few minutes, until the liquid has reduced by a third. Add bay leaves and thyme. Heat over a gentle flame, add butter and stir from time to time. After about five minutes, strain the sauce. Just before serving, add three ounces of chopped beef marrow with the juice of a lemon.

This is all very well. The Decadent will no doubt be attracted to such recipes, not least for their capacity to *épater la bourgeoisie*. However, the true Decadent will not be content with that. He will wish to go further. His yearning for the bizarre and the exotic will constantly lead him to explore more and more remote culinary regions. One of the regions which should attract the Decadent is that of endangered species.

To begin with, there is an appeal in the sheer perversity of such an endeavour. Imagine being presented with the last Dodo, stuffed and roast. Would the Decadent not find a certain piquancy to the flavour, knowing that he was condemning an entire species to extinction? Would not every bite be savoured to the full, knowing that nobody would ever be able to prepare this dish again? It would be not only an experience of great intensity but also a moment of great solemnity.

And consider the public loathing and universal opprobrium which would be heaped on one who was discovered to have engaged in something so unspeakable! This would merely add to the true Decadent's delight. He would show nothing but scorn for such pious and sentimental opinions. Nature and the Natural are something to be abhorred and avoided. They are as unappealing to the Decadent as the countryside. As that famous dandy, the Comte de St Médard famously remarked: "*I hate war. Why? Because it always takes place in the countryside and I hate the countryside.*"

The following are suggestions for dishes which require animals teetering on the edge of extinction. But first, *verbum sapienti!* Many of these creatures live in dangerous and out-of-the-way places. We strongly advise that you remain at home in the comfort of your own drawing room while others are engaged in the hunting and capture of them.

Let us begin with the aye-aye. This creature is to be found on the island of Madagascar in the Indian Ocean. It is a relative of the lemur and only about 20 of them remain in the wild. The following is an adaptation of a recipe for squirrel, which was devised by Viscount Weymouth's housekeeper.

FOR A MOULD:

1 AYE-AYE

2 CARROTS

1 ONION

$1/2$ RED PEPPER

SALT AND PEPPER

1 CUP OF DRY CIDER

ASPIC

FOR THE SAUCE:

1 TEASPOON OF OIL

2 TEASPOONS TOMATO PURÉE

1 TABLE SPOON SINGLE CREAM

SALT AND PEPPER

$1/2$ CUP OF DRY CIDER

Having skinned and gutted the aye-aye, steam it until the meat comes away from the bone. Allow to cool. Slice the carrots and pepper and chop the onion. Grease as many portions of an egg poacher as needed. Put a layer of aye-aye meat, onion, carrot and pepper into the poacher. Place another layer of meat on top. Season with salt and pepper and add a little dry cider. Poach until the vegetables are tender, about half an hour, and leave to cool. Mix the aspic and cider, pour into the poachers and allow to set. Combine all the sauce ingredients and pour over the aye-aye moulds when you turn them out.

ROAST IBIS WITH CHAWDRON SAUCE

Fewer than a dozen Japanese Ibis are thought to have survived the destruction of their breeding grounds. As they are wading birds, the flavour might be a little fishy, but no more so than, say, a heron. The following recipe may well suit the Ibis.

Cut its neck and collect the blood. Skin it, cut off the neck, feet and wings. Roast the bird and baste it with lard.

As an accompaniment, we suggest Chawdron sauce. One J. Russell, writing in 1460, states: *To signet and swann, convenyent is the chawdoun* . Recommendation enough! The method is as follows: Take the innards of the bird and cut them into small pieces. Clean and boil in water. Mix some of the liquid with bread, ginger powder and galingale. (If you have run out of galingale the ginger will suffice). Strain the mixture and add the blood and salt. This in turn is combined with the innards after they have been strained. Bring the sauce to the boil and add vinegar to taste.

KAPOKO PIE

The parrot owl of New Zealand, also known as the kapako, has been hunted to the point where it is almost extinct, so presumably it is rather tasty. Mrs Beeton provided the following recipe - originally for parakeets.

Ingredients: 2 kapakos, a few slices of beef (underdone cold beef is the best for this purpose) 4 rashers of bacon, 3 hard-boiled eggs, minced parsley and lemon peel, pepper and salt, stock, puff paste.

Mode: Fillet and joint the birds. Line a pie-dish with the beef cut into slices, over them place the breasts and legs of one of the kapakos, dredge with flour, fill up the spaces with the eggs cut into slices and scatter over the seasoning. Next put the bacon, cut in small strips, then kapako and fill up with beef seasoning as well. Pour in the stock and water to nearly fill the dish, cover with puff paste and bake for one hour.

ROAST THYLACINE

The Tasmanian wolf or thylacine was thought to be extinct, but according to a recent expedition, its footprints have been spotted, so this marsupial may still be around. It provides the best candidate so far for that coveted 'last of the species' dish. This recipe is also based on an Eliza Beeton recipe, this time for wallaby.

Ingredients: 1 thylacine, forcemeat, milk, butter.

In winter the animal may hang for some days, as a hare, but in summer it must, like all other flesh, be cooked very soon after it is killed. Cut off the hindquarters at the first joints and after skinning and paunching, let it lie in water for a while to draw out the blood. Make a good veal forcemeat, and after well washing the inside of the creature, stuff it and sew it up. Truss as a hare and roast before a bright clear fire from one and a quarter to one and three-quarter hours according to size. It must be kept some distance from the fire when first put down, or the outside will be too dry before the inside is done. Baste well, first with milk and then with butter, and when nearly done, dredge with flour and baste again with butter until nicely frothed.

PANDA PAW CASSEROLE

For centuries, the front feet of the bear have been considered the choicest part of the animal. The Chinese hold them in high esteem, and in Germany, where they particularly enjoy cub meat, the front paws are a great delicacy, for those who can afford them.

This recipe was given by M. Urbain Dubois, chef to their Majesties of Prussia during the last century. We have added a small but important adaptation - our recipe specifies Giant Panda paws. Start by skinning the paws. (There was a time of course when one could buy bear paws already skinned. Alas, no longer.) Then wash them, salt them, put them in a terrine and cover them with a marinade cooked with vinegar, in which they are left to steep for two or three days.

Line a casserole with bacon, ham trimmings and vegetables. Lay the paws on the vegetables, cover them with marinade, some bouillon and some thin slices of bacon. Leave it to cook for seven or eight hours on a very low heat. Add liquid as it reduces. When the paws are cooked, leave them in the liquid until they are almost cold. Then drain and wipe them before cutting them lengthways in four. Sprinkle them with cayenne pepper before rolling them first in lard and then in breadcrumbs. Grill them gently for half an hour. Arrange them in a platter on top of a piquant sauce (reduced, with two spoonfuls of currant jelly added as a finishing touch).

What one does with the rest of the bear is beyond the scope of this particular book.

LABELS

by Louis de Bernières

I was brought up in the days when there was electric light but no television, and consequently people had to learn how to amuse themselves. It was the great heyday of hobbies. People made entire villages out of matchboxes, and battleships out of matches. They made balsa aeroplanes, embroidered cassocks with coats of arms and scenes of the martyrdom of saints, and pressed flowers. My grandfather knitted his own socks, made wooden toys, cultivated friendships with spiders in his garden shed, cheated at croquet, and learned how to produce his own shot-gun cartridges. My grandmother's hobby was flower-arranging and social climbing, and my mother played spirituals on the piano in between sewing new covers for the furniture and knitting woolly hats for the deserving poor. My uncle rolled his own cigars from tobacco grown and cured by himself. My other grandmother spent happy hours in the garden collecting slugs that she could drop down the grating outside the kitchen, and below a hoard of portly toads would eat them before hiding themselves once more beneath the accumulation of dead leaves.

My two sisters had a hobby called 'dressing up'. It consisted of emptying the trunks in the attic, and draping themselves in the extraordinary clothes inherited from previous generations. Then they would go out in the street, posing as indigent old ladies, and beg coins from passers-by. One of my sisters, I forget which one, actually managed to wheedle a florin from our own mother, who failed to recognise her. We spent the florin on jamboree bags, sherbet fountains, and those dangerous fireworks called 'jumping jacks'. We set them off all at once in a field of cows, and sat on the gate gleefully watching the ensuing stampede. It was only me who got spanked for it, however, since little girls in those days were not judged to be capable of such obviously boyish mischief.

As for me, I evolved through a series of pastimes, which began as a toddler. My first hobby was saying good morning. I had a little white floppy hat that I would raise to anyone at any time of day, in imitation of the good manners of my father, and I would solemnly intone 'good morning' in a lugubrious tone of voice that I had probably first admired in a vicar. After that I developed an interest in drains, and would squat before them, poking with a stick at the limp shreds of apple peel and cabbage that had failed to pass through the grate outside the kitchen. I noticed that in the autumn the leaves turned grey, and I discovered the miraculous binding quality of human hair when it is intermixed with sludge. From this I progressed naturally to a brief fascination with dog manure, and am perplexed to this day as to why it was that occasionally one came across a little pile that was pure white. Nowadays one never sees such faecal albinism. My wife recalls that as a child she had assumed that such deposits were made by white poodles.

As infancy blossomed into childhood, so my interests multiplied. I made catapults, tormented the cat, pretended to be a cowboy, made boxes with air-holes so that I could watch caterpillars become chrysalides, made a big collection of model biplanes and Dinky cars, amassed conkers, marbles, seagull feathers, and the squashy bags in the centre of golf balls. At one point I became interested in praying, and knelt quite often over the graves of our pet animals.

The morbidity of adolescence was to provide me with new joys, such as taxidermising dead animals and suffering relentless hours of torment from being agonisingly in love with several untouchable girls all at the same time. I read every Biggles book I could find, read Sir Walter Scott novels without realising that they were classics, memorised hundreds of filthy limericks and rugby songs that I can still recite faultlessly, and discovered that it was possible to have wet dreams whilst still wide awake.

Many of my friends pursued arcane hobbies, such as collecting cigarette cards and cheese wrappers, shrinking crisp packets in the oven, train and bus spotting, egg-blowing, origami, inspecting each other's endowments behind clumps of bamboo, collecting African stamps, and farming garden snails in a vivarium. One of my friends made a hobby of moles, and carved perfect representations of them in softwood with the aid of a scalpel.

Another collected one hundred and fifty pairs of wings from small birds that he had shot with an air-rifle. He then suffered a crisis of conscience and joined the Royal Society for the Protection of Birds, becoming eventually one of the few people in this country to have spotted a Siberian warbler, which was unfortunately eaten by a sparrowhawk before the horrified eyes of thirteen twitchers concealed in one small hide.

Like everyone else I was reduced to extreme torpor and inactivity by the advent of television, but found that I was becoming increasingly depressed and irritable. After a couple of years I realised that I was suffering from the frustration of having no interests in life, and searched around for something to do.

I was in our corner-shop one day when I was most forcibly struck by the appealing eyes of a cat depicted on the label of a tin of catfood, and it occurred to me that a comprehensive collection of catfood labels might one day be of considerable interest to historians of industry, and that to be a connoisseur of catfood labels would surely be a sufficiently rare phenomenon for me to be able to become an eminent authority in a comparatively short time. Instantly I dismissed the idea from my mind as intrinsically absurd, and returned home.

An hour later however, I was mocking myself at the same time as I was buying the tin with the appealing picture of the cat. With the tin comfortingly weighing down the pocket of my jacket on one side, I returned home once more, and eagerly lowered it into a pan of hot water so that I could soak off the label. I wrecked it completely by trying to peel it off before the glue had properly melted, and had to go out to buy another tin. This time I waited for the paper to float free of the can, and carefully hung it up on the line that I had stretched from a hot water pipe in one corner of the kitchen over to a hook that I had screwed into the frame of the window. I went out to the stationer's and bought a photograph album and some of those little corner pockets which are sticky on only one side. I walked restlessly about the house all evening, waiting for the label to dry, and then could not sleep all night for getting up every ten minutes to go and test it with my fingers. In the morning, my eyes itching with tiredness, I glued the label into my album, and wrote the date underneath in white ink.

Afterwards I went out and bought a hair-dryer and two more cans of catfood.

I was to discover that different manufacturers have different methods of securing their labels. The easiest ones to get off are those which are glued with only one blob, relying on the rim of the can and their tight fit to keep them in place, and the worst ones are those which are stuck in place by means of large smears at every ninety degrees. On some of them the glue is so weak that one can peel it off immediately, without soaking, and others have to be immersed in white spirit. I made a comprehensive chart in order to determine at a glance the best methods of removing the labels.

I began to accumulate an embarrassment of delabelled tins, which grew unmanageable just as soon as I realised that one can obtain them in vast sizes, as well as in the smaller sizes that one commonly finds in supermarkets. I rebelled against the wasteful idea of simply throwing them away, and took to giving them away to friends who possessed cats. They were very suspicious at first, and were reluctant to give the food to their pets in case it turned out to be adulterated, or was in fact steamed pudding, or whatever. They soon came round to the idea, however, when the offerings were unspurned by their cats, as did the owners of the cat kennels, to whom I gave the industrial-sized cans. I did notice that many of these people were beginning to look at me askance, as though I were a little mad, and it is the truth that I stopped receiving invitations to dinner parties because my conversation had become monomaniac. I think the worst thing was when my wife left me, saying that she would not consider coming back until I had removed all the albums from her side of the bedroom. The house became a terrible tip because I had had no experience of doing the housework, and eventually I had to pay her to come back once a week in order to dust and tidy.

It occurred to me that the easiest way of obtaining labels would be to write to petfood companies and request samples, past and present, but I received no co-operation at all. My first replay was similar to all the others, and ran like this:

Dear Sir,

Our manager asks me to thank you for your kind letter, and assures you that it is receiving his closest attention.

With best wishes to you and your pussy, we remain, yours sincerely...

Having received this letter, I would hear nothing more.

It may surprise many people to know that the variety of catfood labels is virtually infinite. To begin with, every manufacturer changes the label fairly frequently in order to modify the targeting of the customer, and to attempt to gain an edge over other brands. Thus a brunette might be changed to a blonde to make a particular food more glamorous, and a Persian cat might be substituted for a ginger moggy in order to give an impression of high class. Shortly afterwards the woman might be changed to a beautiful Asian in order to appeal to the burgeoning immigrant market, and the cat be changed to a tabby to give it a no-nonsense, no-woofters-around-here, working-class appeal. The labels are often changed by the addition of 'special offer' announcements, or, most annoyingly, by 'free competitions' where the competition is on the back of the label so that one has to buy two cans the same in order to have both the obverse and the front of the sticker in one's album.

In addition, every supermarket has its own brand, and every manufacturer is constantly adding to the range, so that, whereas in the old days there was just Felix, Whiskas, Top Cat, etc., each one now has flavours such as rabbit and tuna, quail, salmon, pigeon, truffles, and calf liver, each one with changing labels as detailed above. Everyone knows that the food is mostly made of whales slaughtered by the Japanese for 'scientific research', cereals, French horses, exhausted donkeys, and bits of the anatomy of animals that most people would prefer not to eat, but recently the producers have cottoned on to the fact that cat owners tend to buy the food that their cat likes the most, and consequently have introduced greater and greater quantities of finer meat, so that indeed one finds real pieces of liver and genuine lumps of rabbit.

It was when my collection began to go international that I hit the financial rocks. I had been working for several years as a bailiff, a job to which I was well suited on account of my great size and my ability to adopt an intimidating expression. I had managed to remain afloat by cutting expenses wherever possible; my house was falling apart, my garden was a wilderness, my car was ancient, I had bought no new clothes for five years, and I cut my own hair with the kitchen scissors. I once sat down with my albums and worked out that I had spent the equivalent of two years' salary on catfood. But I was not broke.

What brought everything to a crisis was a trip to France in pursuit of a debt defaulter. I stopped off in a Champion supermarket, and, whilst looking for a tin of cassoulet, I happened upon rows and rows of catfood with beautiful labels, many of them in black, with distinguished scrolly writing on them. It was love at first sight, and I bought every single type I could find, not just there, but in every Mamouth and Leclerc supermarket that I passed. I broke the back axle on the way home, and my hoard of tins eventually arrived by courtesy of the Automobile Association's relay service.

Naturally it became worse and more disastrous by the month. I made frequent weekend trips to France, and returned burdened with cans of Luxochat, Poupouche and Minette Contente. Thereafter I took sick leave from work and discovered the treasure trove of Spain. Not for me the Alhambra; it was Señorito Gatito, Minino, Micho Miau and Ronroneo.

I came home bursting with happiness and *joie de vivre*, planning to cover Germany, and found that my world had fallen apart. My skiving had been discovered, and I was fired from my job, at exactly the same time that I received final demands for electricity, the gas, the telephone, and a reminder to pay my television licence. I sat amongst my albums and my pile of Spanish cans, and realised that I had allowed myself to drift into disaster. I beat myself about the head, first with my hands, and then with rolled up newspaper. I raised my eyes to the heavens in exasperation, moaned, rocked upon my haunches, and smashed a dinner plate on the kitchen floor. Pulling myself together, I made an irrevocable decision to destroy my entire collection.

Out in the garden I built a sizeable bonfire out of garden waste and my old deck-chairs, and went indoors to collect the albums. I found myself flicking through them. I thought, 'Well, I might just keep that one, it's the only Chinese one I've got', and 'I'll not throw that one away, it's a Whiskas blue from ten years ago', or 'That was the last one I got before my wife left. It has sentimental value.' Needless to say, I didn't burn any of them; I just got on with soaking off the labels on the Spanish cans.

My unemployment benefit did not even begin to cover my personal expenses as well as the cost of acquiring new tins, and I was reduced to buying stale loaves from the baker, and butcher's bones with which to make broth. I had to slice the bread with a saw, and would attempt to extract the marrow from the bones with a large Victorian corkscrew. I became demented with hunger, and the weight fell off me at a rate equalled only by the precipitate loss of my hair from extreme worry. One day, in desperation, I opened one of my tins, sniffed the meat, and began to reason with myself.

'It's been sterilised,' I said to myself, 'and a vet told me that it's treated to a higher standard than human food. OK, so it's full of ground testicles, lips, udders, intestines and vulvas, but so are sausages, and you like them. And what about those pork pies that are full of white bits and taste of gunpowder? They don't taste of pork, that's for sure. Besides,' I continued, 'cats are notoriously fussy and dainty eaters, apart from when they eat raw birds complete with feathers, and so if a cat finds this acceptable and even importunes people for it, maybe it's pretty nice.'

I fetched a teaspoon, and dipped the very tip of it into the meat. I raised it to my nose and sniffed. I thought that in truth it smelt quite enticing. I forced myself to place the spoon in my mouth, conquered the urge to retch, and squashed the little lump against my palate. I chewed slowly, and then ran to the sink and spat it out, overwhelmed with disgust. I sat down, consumed with a kind of sorrowful self-hatred, and began to suffer that romantic longing for death that I had not felt since I was a teenager. My life passed before my eyes, and I had exactly the same kind of melancholy reflections about the futility and meaninglessness of existence as I had experienced after Susan Borrowdale refused to go to the cinema with me, and my sister came instead because she felt sorry for me.

But these cogitations were interrupted by a very pleasant aftertaste from my mouth, and by the fact that I was salivating copiously. I picked up the can at my feet, and sniffed it again. 'All it needs,' I said to myself, 'is a touch of garlic, a few herbs, and it would really make a very respectable terrine.'

I took it into the kitchen and emptied it out into a dish. I peeled three cloves of garlic and crushed them. I grated some fresh black pepper and some Herbes de Provence, and mashed the meat with the extra ingredients. I squashed it all into a bowl, levelled it off with a fork, decorated it with three bay leaves, and poured melted butter over it so that it would look like the real thing when it came out of the fridge.

It was absolutely delicious spread over thin toasted slices of stale bread; it was positively a spiritual experience. It was the gastronomical equivalent of making love for the first time to someone that one has pursued for years.

I suffered the indignity of being visited by the same firm of bailiffs for which I used to work, but my old mates were kind to me and took only things that I did not need very much, such as the grandfather clock and my ex-wife's Turkish carpet. They left me my fridge, my cooker, my collection of books on the manufacture of terrines and pâtés, my vast accumulation of garlic crushers, peppermills, herbs and French cast-iron cookware. I never could do things by halves, I always had to have complete collections.

I became extremely good at my new vocation. The more expensive catfoods made exquisite coarse pâtés and meat pies (my shortcrust pastry is quite excellent, and I never leave big gaps filled up with gelatine, like most pie-makers). The cheaper ones that have a lot of cereal generally do not taste very good unless they are considerably modified by the addition of, for example, diced mushroom and chicken livers fried in olive oil. Turkey livers are a little too strong and leave a slightly unpleasant aftertaste.

The fish-based catfoods are generally very hard to use. With the exception of the tuna and salmon, they always carry the unmistakable aroma of catfood, which is caused, I think, by the overuse of preservatives and flavour-enhancers. They are also conducive to lingering and intractable halitosis, as any owner of an affectionate cat will be able to confirm.

And so this is how catfood, which got me into so much

trouble, also got me out of it. I began by supplying the local delicatessen, and was surprised to find that I was able to make over one hundred per cent profit. I redoubled my efforts, and learned to decorate my products with parsley and little slices of orange. I learned the discreet use of paprika, and even asafoetida. This spice smells of cat ordure, but is capable of replacing garlic in some recipes, and in that respect it is similar to Parmesan cheese, which, as everyone knows, smells of vomit but improves the taste of minced meat.

I also discovered that the addition of seven-star Greek brandy is an absolute winner, and this led me on to experiments with calvados, Irish whiskey, kirsch, armagnac, and all sorts of strange liquors from Eastern Europe and Scandinavia.

But what really made the difference was printing the labels in French, which enabled me to begin to supply all the really expensive establishments in London: *Terrine de Lapin à l'Ail* sounds far more sophisticated than 'Rabbit with Garlic', after all. I had some beautiful labels printed out, in black, with scrolly writing.

I have become very well-off, despite being a one-man operation working out of my own kitchen, and I am very contented. I have outlets in delicatessens and restaurants all over Britain, and one in Paris, and my products have even passed quality inspections by the Ministry of Agriculture and Foods. It might be of interest to people to know that my only complete failure was duck pâté that was not made of catfood at all.

I go out quite often on trips across Europe, looking for superior brands of catfood with nice labels, and my ex-wife often comes with me, having moved back in as soon as I became successful. She had become most skilful at soaking off labels, and is a deft hand with an *hachoir*. The liver with chives was entirely her own invention, and she grows most of our herbs herself.

I recently received two letters which greatly amused me. One was from a woman in Bath who told me that my terrines are 'simply divine' and that her blue-point Persian pussycat 'absolutely adores them' as well.

The other was from a man who said that he was beginning a collection of my 'most aesthetically pleasing' labels, and did I have any copies of past designs that I could send to him? I wrote back as follows:

Dear Sir,

Our manager thanks you for your letter and asks me to assure you that it is receiving his closest attention.

Naturally I never wrote back again, nor did I send him any labels. None the less I feel a little sorry for him, and anxious on his behalf; it's easy enough to turn catfood into something nice, but what do you do with hundreds of jars of pâté? With him in mind, I had a whole new range of labels printed in fresh designs, with details of a competition on the reverse.

Labels, Louis de Bernières.

Louis de Bernières is a novelist who lives in London. His works to date are *The War of Don Emmanuel's Nether Parts, Señor Vivo and the Coca Lord, The Troublesome Offspring of Cardinal Guzman* and *Captain Corelli's Mandolin* (all published by Minerva, London). The short story 'Labels' was published in the British Council anthology *New Writing 4* (Vintage, London, 1995).

CHAPTER 8

THE DECADENT SAUSAGE

Take pigs' throats and cut out the fat, but keep the clean, smooth glands. Slice the loins finely; also the ears (well scoured), and the snouts; peel the tongues and wash them thoroughly in hot water; bone, scrub and singe the trotters; clean the testicles. Lay the ears, snouts and trotters on the bottom of a good clean pot and cover with coarse salt. On top put the tongues, then the throats, loins and testicles sprinkled with fine salt. Let the pot stand for three days then swill out with red wine. Soak the lot with red wine for another day. Drain, rinse several times to get rid of the salt, and dry with clean white cloths. Pack the ingredients tight into a sausage skin. Use at once or store.

This recipe comes from a cookbook by Christoforo di Messisbugo, chef to the Duke of Este in Parma in the 16th century. They don't make sausages like that any more - in Parma or anywhere else. But if size is what you're after you can still, in Italy, get a massive thing called a *bondola* . It's a kind of *mortadella* - with the weight and dimensions of a 12-inch naval cannon - fatty, pink and rather slimy on the tongue. Sometimes it has emerald pistachios set into its spam-like bulk. It's rough peasant fare, as the cliché goes, and you eat it (when you're extremely hungry) sliced very thick on bread.

Elizabeth David said you could get good *mortadella* in Bologna. (A good one means pure pork, not 'a mixture of pork, veal, tripe, pig's head, donkey meat, potato or soya flour, and colouring essence'.) This was in 1954, but it's probably still true. Italy, just as much as Germany, is good sausage country, and conservative in its cooking habits.

Lucania, in southern Italy, was the place for sausages in ancient times. Apicius, the Roman gastronome, says the ingredients were pork or beef, nuts, parsley, cumin, laurel berries and rue. They were cased in long narrow pieces of intestine and hung in the chimney to smoke. *Lucanicae* was the Latin name, which lives on in Italian *luganeghe* (still long and thin, but unsmoked now) and Greek *loukanika*.

You can make sausages out of practically anything, which

may be why there are six hundred different kinds listed in that great sausage-hunter's bible - Antony and Araminta Hippisley Coxe's *Book of Sausages*. The Roman Emperor Heliogabalus is supposed to have invented the shrimp, crab, oyster, prawn and lobster sausage. Apicius gives a recipe that includes calf's brains and almonds. Eskimos fill sausages with seals' blood and offal. In Arles they use donkey or horse meat, in Madrid a mixture of veal and sardines, in Westphalia the brains of pigs. Traditional recipes boast delicacies such as black bear (Germany), porpoise (England), reindeer (Norway), rabbit (England again), and armadillo (Texas). Postmodernists may like to try another English recipe: Christmas pudding sausages, fried in egg and breadcrumbs and served with brandy butter.

Sausage names can be very poetic. *Larousse Gastronomique* mentions the *Gendarme* - 'very dry and heavily smoked' - which suggests a philosophical detective out of the 1940s. Then there's the *Saucisson Princesse*, made of diced ox-tongue, the *Jagdwurst* (or hunter's sausage), the *Punkersdorker*, 'a strong, juicy German salami', the *Puddenskins*, the *Felino*, the *Black Hog's Pudding*, the *Alpiniste...*

Sausages are also medicinal, which is why great thinkers like Rabelais have always taken them seriously. They operate like wine, tobacco, jokes, sunshine, sex, anchovies, rock'n'roll, etc, according to their own arcane laws, which have nothing to do with the beliefs of men with stethoscopes and white coats. Someone who truly understood the healing power of sausages was that fabulous old queen Madame de Maintenon, wife of Louis XIV. When she and *le roi soleil* were both very antiquated and sinking fast she recorded this touching little digestive swansong:

'I seldom breakfast, and then only on bread and butter. I take neither chocolate, nor coffee, nor tea, being unable to endure these foreign drugs. I am German in all my habits. I eat no soup but such as I can take with milk, wine, or beer. I cannot bear broth - it makes me sick, and gives me the colic. When I take broth alone I vomit even to blood, and nothing can restore the tone of my stomach but ham and sausages.'

Decadents, like clapped-out French monarchs, are always on the look-out for elixirs to restore their rogered constitutions. They should never overlook the sausage. In the words of the writer

Francis Amunatégui, founder of the A.A.A.A.A. (*Association Amicale des Amateurs d'Authentiques Andouillettes*), 'The appearance of a hot sausage with its salad of potatoes in oil can leave nobody indifferent.... It is pure, it precludes all sentimentality, it is the Truth.'

Yellow Sausages

This is a simple restorative sausage with mild aphrodisiac qualities.

10 LB CHOPPED PORK
1 LB GRATED CHEDDAR
1OZ EACH OF CINNAMON, CLOVES, GINGER, NUTMEG
2 OZ PEPPER
PINCH OF SAFFRON
SALT
1 GLASS WHITE WINE

Pound the ingredients in a mortar, then cook gently with the wine until the liquid is absorbed. Fill hog casings with the mixture and tie. Reheat in boiling water for 6 minutes before serving.

Stuffed sow's womb
(A RECIPE FROM ANCIENT ROME)

MINCED PORK, CHICKEN, PHEASANT, RABBIT OR PEACOCK;
GROUND PEPPER
CUMIN, AND RUE
FISH STOCK
PEPPERCORNS
PINE NUTS
1 SOW'S WOMB
2 SMALL LEEKS
ANISEED OR DILL

Mix the meat, ground pepper, cumin and rue, and grind very thoroughly. Then pound in a mortar until very fine. Add peppercorns and pine-nuts. Wash the sow's womb very carefully and fill with the stuffing. Cook in olive oil, water and stock, with leeks and aniseed or dill.

Frankfurters Flambés

6 LB FRANKFURTERS

3 LB MUSHROOMS SLICED

6 CLOVES GARLIC

1 LB BUTTER

6 TABLESPOONS CHOPPED PARSLEY

PEPPER

3 TEASPOONS SALT

RATHER A LOT OF CALVADOS OR BRANDY FOR BURNING

Quarter the frankfurters longitudinally and fry them gently in butter for 5 minutes. Add crushed garlic, mushrooms, salt and pepper. Stir and cook for 5 minutes, then add parsley. Climb into asbestos apron, pour on a generous amount of calvados and set the whole thing flaming magnificently before your astonished guests. Serves 20.

A Victorian Sausage
(Mrs Beeton, 1861)

1 LB OF PORK FAT AND LEAN, WITHOUT SKIN OR GRISTLE

1 LB OF LEAN VEAL

1 LB OF BEEF SUET

$1/2$ LB OF BREADCRUMBS

THE RIND OF HALF A LEMON

SOME NUTMEG

6 SAGE LEAVES

1 TEASPOONFUL OF PEPPER

2 TEASPOONSFUL OF SALT

Chop the pork, veal and suet finely together, add the breadcrumbs, lemon peel (which should be well minced) and a grating of nutmeg. Wash and chop the sage leaves very finely. Add these with the remaining ingredients to the sausage-meat and when thoroughly mixed either put the meat into skins, or when wanted for table, form it into little cakes, which should be floured and fried.

BLUE SAUSAGE

A Swiss product, and very handy for snacks to go with curaçao cocktails. Next time you're in Switzerland, buy some! Blue sausages make a less boring present than gold bars full of chocolate, and they don't burst out of their wrappings every hour to squawk 'Cuckoo!'

Why is the blue sausage made in Switzerland? Because the Council of State in Geneva decided in 1903 that all sausages made with horsemeat should be dyed blue.

HOT LIGHTNING

A recipe from Holland. The name is one of those deep Dutch mysteries which you only begin to fathom after your third glass of genever gin.

2 LB COOKING APPLES

2 LB EATING APPLES

4 LB 4 OZ POTATOES

SALT

CLOVES

12 OZ BLOOD SAUSAGE*, THICKLY CUT

BUTTER

Peel and chop the cooking apples then boil them in shallow water for 20 minutes. Add potatoes and eating apples. Continue cooking until all are soft (about half an hour). Add salt and a few cloves, and mash the lot. Keep the mash warm while you fry the blood sausage in butter. Stir the butter and melted fat from the frying into the mash, lay the sausage decoratively on top, and serve.

* for blood sausage recipes see below and 'Blood, the Vital Ingredient'

THE TARPORLEY HUNT BLACK PUDDING

The Black Pudding is a gift to Decadent cuisine. This version is consumed by the Tarporley Hunt Club at their annual dinner, held at the Swan Hotel, Tarporley, Cheshire, in the first week of November. The Club, founded in 1762 and limited to 40 members, keeps its own wine-cellar, china and 18th century mahogany chairs carved with foxes' masks. The Club historian describes the scene: 'The Hunt Room, with its fine portraits and magnificent chandelier, forms a unique setting for the dinners, at which the members wear scarlet coats with green collars, green breeches and green silk stockings. Naturally enough, "Foxhunting" is the principal toast of the evening and, after the speeches, the tables are reset for supper. At about midnight [4 a.m. according to less official sources], devilled bones and black puddings are always served, washed down with mulled ale.'

Several useful tips for Decadent diners here - the silk stockings, the furniture, the timing, 'dinner' followed by 'supper' - not forgetting the whole pretext for the night's revelry - "Foxhunting" - which can be relied on to cause offence right across the social spectrum. 'Devilled bones' are a nice touch too - they were a well-known rouser of flagging thirsts among 18th century voluptuaries. Instructions for making these follow the Black Pudding recipe below.

14 LB GROATS (I.E. HULLED GRAINS OF CEREALS)

7 LB LEAF OR BACK FAT IN HALF INCH CUBES

4 LB FINE OATMEAL

2 LB RUSK

2 LB ONIONS

1 GALLON (4.8 LITRES) PIG'S BLOOD

1 OZ MANCU

2 OZ BERGICE (DRY ANTISEPTIC)

WIDE HOG CASINGS

SEASONING

12 OZ SALT

6 OZ WHITE PEPPER

4 OZ GROUND CORIANDER

3 OZ GROUND PIMENTO

2 OZ CARAWAY SEED

Put the groats into a bag and tie. Boil until swollen and thoroughly cooked. Pour into a tub, add seasonings, bergice, rusk and onions and mix well. Add the fat then the blood and oatmeal. Fill the casings, allowing about four pieces of fat to each pudding. Tie up tightly and boil gently for 20 minutes. For a rich black colour, add 1 oz of *mancu* to the ingredients.

DEVILLED BONES
(TO ACCOMPANY BLACK PUDDING)

A COLD JOINT OF MEAT

ENGLISH MUSTARD POWDER MADE UP WITH WORCESTER

SAUCE OR CHILLI VINEGAR

BUTTER

DEVIL PEPPER (1 TEASPOON EACH OF FRESHLY GROUND

BLACK PEPPER, SALT, & CAYENNE PEPPER)

Cut the meat into pieces and dip in the mustard. Dot with butter and sprinkle with devil pepper, then grill furiously until scorched and crisp.

WEST INDIAN BLACK PUDDING

This achieves the amazing feat of making black pudding seem tropical and exotic rather than an emanation of grey northern skies.

4 TABLESPOONS SALT

1 LIME

2 SPRING ONIONS

2-3 HOT RED PEPPERS

4 OZ SWEET POTATO (OR COOKED RICE)

2 OZ PUMPKIN

SPRIG OF MARJORAM

BLACK PEPPER

$^1/_4$ PINT PIG'S BLOOD

1 OZ BUTTER

3-4 FT HOG CASING

Chop the spring onions and crush the peppers. Peel and grate the sweet potato and the pumpkin and mix with the onions, peppers, marjoram, salt and black pepper. Strain in the pig's blood and stir well. Fill the intestine and tie off leaving 1 inch for expansion. Join the two ends to form a circle, place in boiling water and simmer for 20 minutes. Then prick the skin to prevent bursting. Cook gently for a further 30 minutes and serve hot.

ANDOUILLES AND ANDOUILLETES

The great beauty of these French sausages is that they consist of guts inside guts. As a culinary-aesthetic concept this scores highly. The taste is also a revelation. The *andouillette* is made from chitterling (the middle section of a pig's intestines) or calf mesentery (a membrane covering part of the intestines) and tripe. It is eaten grilled. The *andouille* adds up to 50% of pork meat. It is fatter and it enters the *salle à manger* in slices.

Perhaps because of their colouring as well as their shape and size, *andouilles* and *andouillettes* can look very phallic. This is something for Decadent cooks to exploit or ignore as they think fit. The resemblance lies behind a popular song in Jargeau ('Capitale de l'Andouille') -

Si t'étais venu, t'aurais mangé de l'andouille,
Comme t'es pas venu, elle est restée pendue.

If you'd come you'd have eaten andouille,
As you didn't, it just hung there.

You can buy *andouilles* and *andouillettes* ready-made from a French pork butcher. Not all Decadents are in a position to do this, however, and as the urge for them (once tasted) can come on very suddenly and strong, here are some simple instructions:

ANDOUILLETTES

A CALF MESENTERY

A HEIFER'S UDDER (TROYES VARIANT)

CHITTERLING AND TRIPE (SAVOIE VARIANT)

HALF THE COMBINED WEIGHT OF THESE IN LEAN BACON

THYME, BAY LEAF, BOUQUET GARNI

PARSLEY (CUMIN FOR SAVOIE, NUTMEG FOR TROYES)

1 LITRE STOCK (MADE PARTLY WITH WINE IF YOU WISH)

1 ONION STUDDED WITH CLOVES

4 OZ MUSHROOMS, SLICED

3 SHALLOTS, CHOPPED

6 EGG YOLKS

CASINGS

Cut the meat into small squares. Simmer in stock with herbs and onion for 2 hours. Cook mushrooms and shallots gently in butter, then add parsley (or cumin or nutmeg). Take the meat out of the stock and chop it coarsely. Boil the stock fast to reduce it. Bind the other ingredients with the egg yolks, then mix with the stock and fill the casings to make sausages 5 inches long. Salt in brine for 48 hours, or hang in smoke for 3 days, or cook in a bouillon of wine and water or milk and water (50/50) for a further 30 minutes.

To serve: slash diagonally a few times and grill on both sides. Garnish with mustard and potatoes, puréed celery, apples or red cabbage. If in Strasbourg, surround with *sauerkraut*. A more extravagant method *(à la tourangelle)* is to souse the *andouillettes* in

Armagnac for 24 hours, fill a buttered dish with sliced mushrooms sprinkled with lemon juice, lay the *andouillettes* on top, add salt, pepper and a glass of Vouvray, and cook in a blazing oven for 40 minutes, turning and basting from time to time.

La 'nduia come si fa a Spilinga

———•◦•———

Spilinga is a small grey hillside town in the far south of Italy where a unique sausage is made. Prepared from 'the worst parts of the pig and the best parts of the pepper', it's a fiery concoction renowned for its capacity to scour the arteries, purge the intestines and exhilarate the sexual organs. Its bulging red balloons lie on Calabrian salami counters daring you to make their day. They look homicidal - but it's all swagger and bluff. Once eaten they sit sweetly inside you, spreading warmth, well-being, genial effusions, lust, etc.

The 'nduia is a mixing or spreading sausage. You mix it in with a plate of pasta, or smear it like mustard on grilled meat. You can even spread it on toast. The name sounds very like the French *andouille* , but the ingredients are as different as can be. This recipe comes from Tino Pugliese of Spilinga, musicologist, gourmet and expert 'nduia maker.

70 LB LOWEST QUALITY MEAT FROM A PIG - THE WINDPIPE,

FAT PARTS OF THE BELLY, NECK, ETC.

10 LB HOT RED PEPPERS

20 LB SWEET RED PEPPERS

3 LB SALT

HOG CASINGS - NARROW, MEDIUM, AND WIDE

Buy the peppers in late summer, and dry them slowly on strings in a well-ventilated place for 2-3 months. They should not be too dry and still have a little flesh left on them when you use them. In early December, at pig slaughtering time, take all the least prized pieces of meat, the left-overs from bacon, sausage and salami making, and mince them as finely as possible. Seed the peppers and mince them finely too.

Mix the meat and peppers with the salt and knead on a board for 15 minutes. Cut the casings into 15 inch lengths, tie one end of each with string, leaving a loose end of about 3 feet of string. Stuff in the mixture, packing it tight. Form into links 6 inches long and tie them off with slip-knots. Fasten the top ends and hang 6 feet above a slow, smoky fire in a room where the air can circulate. Let them smoke for 2 hours per day for a week. Smoke again as necessary in damp weather. Use the narrow 'nduia for immediate consumption (up to March-April), medium for April to July, wide for July onwards.

When the 'nduia is ready, try a forkful on a plate of *spaghetti alla carbonara, alla matriciana, al ragù,* or any other dish you fancy. Also good with melon.

B L A C K   B E A R   S A U S A G E S

Now that the mountain ranges of Eastern Europe have been re-opened to the huntsman, we can hope that black bear sausages will regain their rightful place on the breakfast chariots of the West. The best sausage bears are males 12-18 months old, shot in the autumn. Be warned, though: bears are dangerous, rare and unpredictable. A German businessman on a recent hunting trip to Hungary fell into the hands of a wily 'peasant guide' who, knowing there were no bears left in the wild, bought an old performing bear from a circus and released it into the woods a few hundred metres from his client. The bear found the woods an unfamiliar and frightening place, and made for the more welcoming surroundings of a village, where it found at last something it recognized: a bicycle. Climbing on, it rode happily round the lanes for a while, until it met the businessman, who got such a shock that he had a heart-attack and died. The story might have ended happily there, with the bear enjoying a bottle of beer and a plate of grilled businessman sausages in the local pub, if the shotgun hadn't gone off in the confusion, causing the bear a fatal heart attack of its own...

So, with the moral of this sobering tale in mind, and taking all appropriate precautions, here are black bear sausages:

$1^3/4$ LB LEAN BEAR MEAT, AND

$1^1/4$ LB SHOULDER OF PORK, BOTH MINCED

2 ONIONS AND 2 CLOVES OF GARLIC, FINELY CHOPPED

BLACK AND WHITE PEPPER

PAPRIKA

A FEW CRUSHED JUNIPER BERRIES

AS A PRESERVATIVE: 1 OZ SALT, $^1/2$ OZ BROWN SUGAR, $^1/4$ OZ

SALTPETRE

HOG CASINGS ($1^1/2$ INCHES WIDE, 12 INCHES LONG)

Mix all the ingredients, stuff into casings, and hang in cool smoke for 12 hours.

THURINGIAN SAUSAGES
WITH RICE PUDDING

Thuringia in eastern Germany has a high reputation for its sausages, so if you can get them, do. Otherwise this old family recipe can be made with any good frying sausage.

SAUSAGES

RICE PUDDING

Fry the sausages, and serve on a bed of rice pudding. Jam makes an optional garnish.

KROMESKI

'The kromeski or Polish croquette,' says *Kettner's Book of the Table*, 'is made in the usual way with an addition. It is any croquette formed into a little roll and wrapped round with a thin slice of the udder of veal, or failing that with thin bacon. The veal udder (which is always best) or the bacon is boiled beforehand, is then sliced and wrapt round the croquette, which is finally dipped into batter and consigned to the frying-pan, from which it should come out crisp. This is the most seductive of all the forms of croquette.'

ATTERAUX VICTORIA

This is really a dessert kebab rather than a sausage, but the shape is right and the idea ingenious.

Peel and cut apples into $^1/_2$ inch thick circles, 1 inch across, and soak in rum. Cut some cold Christmas pudding into 1 inch discs. Thread Christmas pudding and apples alternately on skewers, packing them tight to form a sausage shape. Dip in egg and breadcrumbs, fry in very hot fat, and serve with brandy butter.

PORPOISE SAUSAGES

A fifteenth century English recipe which speaks for itself:
'Take the blood of him and the grease of himself, and oatmeal and salt and pepper and ginger, mix these well together and then put this into the gut of the porpoise and then let it seethe easily, and not too hard, a good while; and then take him out and broil him a little and then serve forth.'

PRESSWURST

Probably the most offensive sausage in the world.

2 LB STREAKY, PICKLED FORELEG OF PORK

3 LB PIG'S HEAD MEAT

1 LB SALTED PIG'S TONGUE

2 LB SALTED PORK RIND AND CALVES' FEET

STRONG STOCK, PEPPER, SALT, NUTMEG

CORIANDER AND SHALLOTS

Cut the pickled foreleg, the head meat and the tongue into pieces the size of beechnuts. Then add the rind and calves' feet, mix well and chop down to size of peas. Work the mixture together, binding with strong stock. Add the seasoning and fill loosely into a pig's stomach. Simmer for one and a half to two hours.

PUDDENSKINS
A DIALECT RECIPE FROM CORNWALL

'Some brave, big slices of taties, turmuts and onions, all mixed together with pepper and salt and put in a pie dish with a tidy piece of flesh from Mawther's Bussa. Put 'em to cooky, and have some skins (same as they do have for Hogs Puddens) and mix flour, suet, oatmeal and figs and an egg, mixen like batter, lookey see! and shove batter into the skins, twist'en round the flesh and cook till light brown. Same to us down-along as Haggis be to they up-along.'

GLOSSARY

turmuts = turnips
flesh from Mawther's Bussa = pork, lightly salted
figs = raisins

ON SUCKING PIG

Charles Lamb on the sucking-pig:

"Of all the delicacies in the whole *mundus edibilis*," he says, "I will maintain it to be the most delicate - *princeps obsoniorum*.

"I speak not of your grown porkers - things between pig and pork - those hobbydehoys; but a young and tender suckling; under a moon old, guiltless as yet of the sty, with no original speck of the *amor immunditiæ*, the hereditary failing of the first parent, yet manifest - his voice as yet not broken, but something between a childish treble and a grumble - the mild forerunner or *præludium* of a grunt.

"*He must be roasted.* I am not ignorant that our ancestors ate them seethed, or boiled - but what a sacrifice of the exterior tegument!

"There is no flavour comparable, I will contend, to that of the crisp, tawny, well-watched, not over-roasted, 'crackling,' as it is well called; the very teeth are invited to their share of the pleasure at this banquet in overcoming the coy, brittle resistance, with the adhesive oleaginous - O call it not fat! but an indefinable sweetness growing up to it - the tender blossoming of fat - fat cropped in the bud, taken in the shoot, in the first innocence - the cream and quintessence of the child-pig's yet pure food: the lean, not lean, but a kind of animal manna, or rather, fat and lean (if it must be so) so blended and running into each other, that both together make but one ambrosian result or common substance.

"Behold him, while he is 'doing': it seemeth rather a refreshing warmth than a scorching heat that he is so passive to. How equably he twirleth round the string! Now he is just done. To see the extreme sensibility of that tender age! - he hath wept out his pretty eyes - radiant jellies, shooting stars!

"See him in the dish, his second cradle: how meek he lieth! Wouldst thou have had this innocent grow up to the grossness and indocility which too often accompany maturer swinehood? Ten to one he would have proved a glutton, a sloven, an obstinate, disagreeable animal, wallowing in all manner of filthy conversation. From these sins he is happily snatched away:

His memory is odoriferous; no clown curseth, while his stomach half rejecteth, the rank bacon; no coalheaver bolteth him in reeking sausages; he hath a fair sepulchre in the grateful stomach of the judicious epicure - and for such a tomb might be content to die.

"Unlike to mankind's mixed characters - a bundle of virtues and vices, inexplicably intertwisted, and not to be unravelled without hazard - he is good throughout. No part of him is better or worse than another. He helpeth, as far as his little means extend, all around. He is the least envious of banquets; he is all neighbours' fare.

"I am one of those who freely and ungrudgingly impart a share of the good things of this life which fall to their lot (few as mine are in this kind) to a friend. . . . But a stop must be put somewhere. One would not, like Lear, 'give everything.' I make my stand upon pig. Methinks it is an ingratitude to the Giver of all good flavours to extra-domiciliate, or send out of the house slightingly (under pretext of friendship, or I know not what), a blessing so particularly adapted - predestined, I may say, to my individual palate. It argues an insensibility.

"Our ancestors were nice in their method of sacrificing these tender victims. We read of pigs whipt to death with something of a shock, as we hear of any other obsolete custom. The age of discipline is gone by, or it would be curious to inquire (in a philosophical light merely) what effect this process might have towards intenerating and dulcifying a substance naturally so mild and dulcet as the flesh of young pigs. It looks like refining a violet. Yet we should be cautious, while we condemn the inhumanity, how we censure the wisdom of the practice. It might impart a gusto.

"I remember an hypothesis, argued upon by the young students, when I was at St. Omer's, and maintained with much learning and pleasantry on both sides, 'Whether, supposing that the flavour of a pig who obtained his death by whipping (*per flagellationem extremam*) superadded a pleasure upon the palate of a man more intense than any possible suffering we can conceive in the animal, is man justified in using that method of putting the animal to death?' I forget the decision.

"His sauce should be considered. Decidedly, a few breadcrumbs, done up with his liver and brains, and a dash of mild sage. But banish, dear Mrs. Cook, I beseech you, the whole onion tribe. Barbecue your whole hogs to your palate, steep them in shallots, stuff them out with plantations of the rank and guilty garlic - you cannot poison them, or make them stronger than they are: but consider, he is a weakling - a flower."

On Sucking Pig, Charles Lamb.

CHAPTER 9

THE MARQUIS DE SADE'S
SWEET TOOTH

It is impossible to talk about Decadence and food without touching on the greatest Decadent of them all - Donatien-Alphonse-François de Sade. Eating was a matter of great importance to the Divine Marquis. His correspondence with his wife is crammed full of requests for food, which is hardly surprising when you consider that he spent most of his adult life - 27 out of his 64 years - behind bars. A letter written from his cell at Vincennes in July 1783 asks Mme de Sade for "... *four dozen meringues; two dozen sponge cakes (large); four dozen chocolate pastille candies - with vanilla - and not that infamous rubbish you sent me in the way of sweets last time.*" The odd delicacy was all he had to look forward to much of the time.

Food played a central role in his fiction too. *Les 120 Journées de Sodome* was described by de Sade as *'l'histoire d'un magnifique repas'*. And the feast laid on by the Comte de Gernande in *La Nouvelle Justine* was typical. It consisted of eighty nine dishes.

'They were served two soups: one Italian pasta with saffron, the other a bisque au coulis de jambon, and between them a sirloin of beef à l'anglaise. There were twelve hors d'oeuvres, six cooked and six raw. Then twelve entrées - four of meat, four of game and four of pâtisseries. A boar's head was served in the middle of twelve dishes of roast meat, which were accompanied by two courses of side dishes, twelve of vegetables, six of different creams, and six of patisseries. There followed twenty fruit dishes or compotes, an assortment of six ice creams, eight different wines, six liqueurs, rum, punch, cinnamon liqueur, chocolate and coffee. Gernande got stuck into all of them. Some of them he polished off on his own. He drank twelve bottles of wine, starting with four Volneys, before moving on to four Ais with the roast meat. He downed a Tokay, a Paphos, a Madeira and a Falernian with the fruit and finished off with two bottles of liqueurs des îles, a pint of rum, two bowls of punch and ten cups of coffee.'

The libertine uses these banquets to stoke up the furnaces of his lust. His ability to eat huge meals is a sign of his sexual prowess. One appetite is connected to the other - and the pleasures of satisfying them are closely allied: *'Après les plaisirs de la luxure,'* says

Gernande, *'il n'en est pas de plus divins que ceux de la table.'* (After the pleasures of lust ... there is none more divine than those of the table.)

But there's also a link between food and cruelty. Gernande again:

J'ai désiré souvent, je l'avoue, d'imiter les débauches d'Apicius, ce gourmand si célèbre de Rome, qui faisait jeter des esclaves vivants dans ses viviers pour rendre la chair de ses poissons plus délicate: cruel dans mes luxures, je le serais tout de même dans ces débauches-là, et je sacrifierais mille individus, si cela était nécessaire, pour manger un plat plus appetisant ou plus recherché.

(I admit that I have often wanted to imitate the debauchery of Apicius, that most famous of Roman gourmets. He had slaves thrown live into his fish ponds so that the flesh of his fish would achieve a greater delicacy. I am cruel in my lusts and would be even more so when it came to such acts of debauchery. I would sacrifice a thousand if necessary, just to eat a dish which was more tempting or recherché.)

The Count's banquet is a prelude to numerous acts of depravity and cruelty, which end with another meal. This is described as *"le plus magnifique souper"* the centre-piece of the table being the body of Gernande's wife, the Comtesse, whom he has bled to death. This doesn't seem to worry his guests unduly, or spoil their appetite.

Although he doesn't actually eat his wife - the Count is more of a vampire than a cannibal - there are, as you might expect, several cannibalistic episodes in the writings of De Sade.

In *Aline et Valcour*, Sainville, in search of his beloved Léonore, arrives in the kingdom of Butua, ruled over by Ben Mâacoro. In this society, captive Jaga tribesmen are eaten piecemeal, sometimes cooked, sometimes raw. When Sainville expresses his moral outrage, Sarmiento, the prime minister, is surprised. *'L'anthropophagie n'est certainement pas un crime,'* he says and justifies the practice in various ways. To begin with, in Butua, young men are simply more tasty than tough old monkey meat. Then, whether a man is buried in the bowels of the earth or the bowels of another man makes no difference. But also, as man forms part of *'le système de la nature'* there is no reason not to eat him just like any other animal. (This brings to mind the story of the Rev. Thomas Baker who took part in an expedition into the interior of Fiji in 1867. He was proudly showing his comb to a local chief, who thought it was a gift and stuck it in his hair as an ornament. Baker brusquely took it back, not realizing that touching a Fijian leader's head was a mortal insult. The chief demanded vengeance. He sent a messenger ahead of Baker on his travels, announcing that a whale's tooth would be the reward for whoever killed him. The mountain tribe at Navatusila took up the offer, killed the Reverend, and cooked him. (Unfortunately the recipe is lost). Most of the tribe enjoyed eating their exotic meal, but those who had been given a leg found that even after lengthy cooking it remained extremely tough. It took some of the more sophisticated islanders to point out that the Wellington boot it wore was not part of the European's skin.)

The argument about the 'naturalness' of cannibalism occurs again in the *Histoire de Juliette* when Juliette and her companions are waylaid by the Russian ogre, Minski. He lives in fabulous wealth in a castle hidden away among the Apennines, not far from the volcanic region of Pietra-Mala. Juliette and the others are invited to dine with him in a room where the tables and chairs are formed by *de groupes de filles artistiquement arrangés*. Seated at this strange furniture the guests are served *plus de vingts entrées ou plats de rôti*. Minski then informs his guests that all the dishes served are human flesh. They overcome any repugnance with phrases like *'il n'est pas plus extraordinaire de manger un homme qu'un poulet'* and tuck in. In true Sadean form, Minski not only eats vast quantities but drinks copiously too; thirty bottles of Burgundy, Champagne with the entremets, Aleatico and Falernian with the dessert. By the end of the meal, more than sixty bottles of wine *étaient entrées dans les entrailles de notre anthropophage*. Again the meal acts as an overture to the most grotesque scenes as the protagonists hurl themselves into the abyss of depravity.

The other cannibal in the *Histoire de Juliette* is Pope Pius VI. Having performed a black mass - itself a form of meal - on the steps of the altar in St Peter's, the Pope 'drunk with lust' tortures and kills an adolescent boy, before tearing out his heart and eating it.

But to return to the man himself, behind bars at Charenton.

Or more precisely, to his wife. Given that she needed to cater for the Marquis' sweet tooth, and wary of providing any more 'infamous rubbish in the way of sweets' Mme de Sade could do no better than turn for help to the sisters of the Santa Trinità del Cancelliere in Sicily. The aristocratic nuns of this Cistercian convent were famous for their *fedde* (sweet cakes, literally 'slices'). These were made in oval-shaped moulds hinged rather like a mussel shell. They were lined with marzipan (*pasta reale*) and filled with apricot jam and egg custard. When one half of the mould was folded over on the other, the filling oozed out and the result looked amazingly like female pudenda.

Another form of *fedde* produced by the nuns were called *Fedde del Cancelliere*. The Chancellor referred to was the 12th century founder of the convent and here *fedde* can mean not only 'slices' but also 'buttocks'.

FEDDE DEL CANCELLIERE
OR CHANCELLOR'S BUTTOCKS

Ingredients for Blancmange filling:

4 CUPS MILK

$^1/_2$ CUP CORNSTARCH

1 $^1/_4$ CUPS SUGAR

$^1/_4$ VANILLA POD

For the dough:

4 CUPS MILK

1 $^1/_2$ CUPS OF SEMOLINA GRANULES

1 $^1/_4$ CUPS SUGAR

4 EGGS

$^1/_2$ VANILLA POD

2 CUPS WHOLE SHELLED PISTACHIOS

1 CUP FLOUR

2 EGGS BEATEN UNTIL FLUFFY

VEGETABLE OIL

$^1/_2$ CUP ICING SUGAR

1 TEASPOON GROUND CINNAMON

Blancmange recipe for Chancellors' Buttocks.

BIANCOMANGIARE PUDDING

$^3/_4$ CUP OF CORNFLOUR

5 CUPS OF MILK

1 CUP OF SUGAR

VANILLA POD

Add the cornflour to a small quantity of milk in a bowl. Make sure the cornflour is dissolved and free of lumps before pouring it into a saucepan with the rest of the milk, the sugar and the vanilla pod. Cook gently, not allowing the milk to boil and stirring constantly, until thick. Remove the vanilla and pour out into a large plate to cool.

For the dough, put the milk, semolina, sugar, eggs, and vanilla into a saucepan. Mix well and heat over a low flame, stirring constantly. Cook until the mixture is very thick and comes away from the side of the pan. Leave it to cool.

Toast the pistachios in a warm oven for 15 minutes and chop very fine.

Remove vanilla pod from dough and stir in pistachios. Shape this into small, buttock-shaped forms about the size of your palm. Dip them in flour and turn them in beaten egg. Put $^1/_4$ inch of oil into a pan and heat. Fry the 'buttocks' in the oil, turning once until delicately browned on each side. Drain on kitchen towel.

Cut the blancmange into 2 in. squares. Split the buttocks like a bun and insert a piece of blancmange into each. Close shut, roll in ground sugar and sprinkle with cinnamon.

The Marquis de Sade might also have enjoyed this sweet Spanish dish. The name means 'Gipsy's arm'.

BRAZO DE GITANO

BUTTER

4 EGGS

6 OZ SUGAR

2 OZ SELF-RAISING FLOUR

WHIPPED CREAM

JAM

BUTTER CREAM OR COFFEE-FLAVOURED CUSTARD

Pre-heat oven to gas mark 5, 375° F.

Grease a large baking tin with butter and dust it with flour. Whisk the eggs and sugar together thoroughly then fold them into the sieved flour. Pour the mixture into a tin and bake in the oven until the sponge is cooked - about 15 minutes. Turn out onto a large sheet of paper sprinkled with icing sugar. Cover it with another piece of paper and roll it up while it is still warm. This helps the roll to keep its shape. Leave it for a few minutes then unroll it and add the coffee custard. Roll it up again and sprinkle the outside with icing sugar, and maybe even a tattoo: *'J'adore ma belle-mère'* in cochineal or indigo...

Turkish cuisine has a number of suggestive dishes. Here are a few for Mme de Sade's basket.

VIRGIN'S BREASTS
(BEKAR GÖGÜS)

---

1 LB KADAYIF PASTRY

(THIS IS SIMILAR TO FILO PASTRY EXCEPT THAT IT IS SHREDDED)

8 OZ UNSALTED BUTTER

12 WALNUT HALVES

3 OZ ALMONDS FINELY CHOPPED

For the syrup:

1 LB 10 OZ SUGAR

450 ML WATER

1 TABLESPOON LEMON JUICE

Preheat the oven to 180° C (350°F) gas mark 4.

It is important to make the Kadayif shreds as fine as possible, which can be done by passing the pastry through a mincer. Drop the pastry into a bowl and then pour most of the melted butter over the top. Mix with your hands until the pastry shreds are covered in the butter.

Next, take a soup ladle (or something of an equivalent shape and size) and lightly butter the inside of it. Put a walnut half at the bottom of the ladle (this will form the nipple), then fill the ladle with shredded pastry and pack it down. Make a hole with your finger in the centre of the pastry, large enough to take 2 teaspoons of chopped nuts. Press the nuts in. Add a little more pastry to act as a plug over the nuts and press down hard to make the pastry firm and solid. Turn the pastry out into your hand and place it on a lightly buttered baking tray. When you have used up all the ingredients in this way, bake the pastries for 40 minutes.

To make the syrup, place the sugar, water and lemon juice in a saucepan and bring to the boil. Simmer for about 10 minutes.

When the pastries are cooked, bring the syrup back to the boil and then spoon some over each one. Set aside to cool. They can be serve on their own or with cream.

LADY'S NAVELS
(KADIN GÖBEGI)

———•◦•———

For the syrup:

1 LB SUGAR

5 ML LEMON JUICE

450 ML WATER

For the dough:

2 OZ BUTTER

$^1/_2$ TEASPOON SALT

8 OZ SIFTED PLAIN FLOUR

3 EGGS

OIL FOR FRYING

1 TEASPOON OF ALMOND ESSENCE

Garnish:

150 ML DOUBLE CREAM WHIPPED

To make the syrup, put the sugar, lemon juice and water in a saucepan and bring to the boil. Simmer for ten minutes then put to one side and allow to cool.

Place the butter and 300 ml of water in a large saucepan and bring to the boil, stirring all the time until the butter melts. Remove from the heat, add the salt and flour and stir vigorously with a wooden spoon until the mixture is well blended. Make a well in the centre of the dough and add the eggs, one at a time. Continue beating until the mixture is smooth, shiny and comes away from the side of the pan.

Lightly oil your hands and break off a piece of dough about the size of an apricot. Roll it between your palms to form a ball. Place on an oiled baking sheet. Carry on until all the dough is used up. Make sure that the balls are well spaced out on the sheet.

Pour 2 inches of oil into the bottom of a large frying pan and heat.

Flatten a few of the balls a little then, after you have dipped your finger in the almond essence, press it into the dough making a depression of about $1/2$ inch. Hence the name of the dish. Place several into the gently sizzling oil fry for 8 minutes on one side before turning and frying for 8 minutes on the other side. The fritters should end up golden brown. Remove with a slotted spoon and allow to drain on some kitchen towel before dropping into the syrup. Turn gently to coat the fritter then leave it to steep for about five minutes. Transfer to a serving dish using a slotted spoon.

Do not let the oil get too hot while you are preparing some more dough balls for frying. Before serving, put a teaspoon of whipped cream into the centre of each fritter.

Alternatively, you can change the shape of the pastries. After you have fashioned the dough into balls, you can flatten them and fold them in two, turning them into '**Beauty's Lips**'.

LADY'S THIGHS
(KADIN BUDU KÖFTE)

1¹/₂ LB OF TWICE MINCED LAMB

1 LARGE ONION

7 OZ COOKED RICE

45 ML. GRATED WHITE CHEESE

1 EGG

1 OZ FLOUR

1¹/₂ TEASPOONS OF SALT

1¹/₂ TEASPOONS BLACK PEPPER

1¹/₂ TEASPOONS GROUND CUMIN

OIL FOR FRYING

1 - 2 BEATEN EGGS

Place all the ingredients in a large bowl and knead for several minutes until the mixture is smooth and well blended. Keeping your hands damp, take a walnut sized lump and roll it into a ball. Flatten it gently by pressing it between your palms. Place on a baking tray and prepare the remaining meat mixture in the same way.

Heat some oil in a large frying pan. Dip a few of the meatballs at a time in beaten egg and fry, turning occasionally, until cooked through and golden. Remove with a slotted spoon, arrange on a serving dish and keep warm while you cook the remaining ones in the same way.

A Dandy's Toothache

by J.K. Huymans

Tonight des Esseintes felt no desire for the taste of music; he contented himself with a small glass of Irish whiskey.

He settled comfortably into his armchair and slowly breathed in the scent of fermented oats and barley; a sharp reek of creosote tarred his mouth.

Bit by bit, as he sipped, his thoughts began to circle around the quickening sensations of his palate, tracking the flavour of the whiskey and reviving memories, through a fatal coincidence of odours, that he had thought long-buried by the years.

The bitter efflorescence of phenol reminded him vividly of a taste that had filled his mouth when dentists last worked on his gums.

His reverie began with a scattered conspectus of all the practitioners he had known; then it converged on just one of them, a character whose eccentric appeal had remained deeply etched in his memory.

It had been three years ago; he had been seized by a violent toothache in the middle of the night. He had stuffed his cheek with wadding and paced up and down his room, banging into the furniture like a madman.

The tooth was a molar that had already been filled. Further repair was out of the question; only a dentist's pliers could kill the pain. He waited feverishly for daylight, ready to face the most excruciating operation as long as it put an end to his sufferings.

Cradling his jaw, he wondered what to do. The dentists who normally treated him were rich businessmen who made appointments at times that suited them. Visits had to be arranged in advance. "It won't do," he said, "I can't put it off any longer". He decided to take his chances with one of the popular tooth-pullers — iron-fisted men who knew nothing of the useless art of patching up holes and drilling away decay, but who could whip out the stubbornest tooth at unrivalled speed. They opened early for business and did not make you wait.

At last the clock struck seven. He rushed out into the street, biting his handkerchief, forcing back tears, thinking of a well-known mechanic who styled himself a cut-price dentist and lived on a corner by the canal.

He reached the house. It was recognizable by a vast black wooden sign where the name GATONAX was painted in enormous pumpkin-yellow letters, alongside two small glass cabinets where rows of plaster teeth nestled in gums made of pink wax, hinged together with brass springs. He panted, sweat bathing his temples. A horrible pang of fear ran through him, shivers raced over his skin; then he grew calmer, the pain eased, the tooth quietened down.

He stood stupidly on the pavement. Finally, steeling himself against his terror, he climbed a dark staircase, four steps at a time, to the third floor. There he found a door where an enamel plaque repeated the name on the sign outside, this time in bright blue letters. He rang the bell, then caught sight of the large red blobs of spittle that splattered the steps; appalled, he made a sudden decision to put up with toothache for the rest of his life; he turned to go, but a piercing shriek tore through the partition walls, filling the stair-well and nailing him in horror to the spot. At the same time the door opened and an old woman asked him to step in.

Shame won the battle with fear; he was led into a dining-room; another door banged open, revealing the ghastly figure of an old soldier, stiff as a board in a black riding-coat and trousers; des Esseintes followed him through to an inner room.

From then on his sensations became confused. He vaguely remembered collapsing into an armchair in front of a window and sputtering, with one finger on his tooth, "It's already been filled; I don't think there's anything you can do."

The man immediately cut short his explanations by poking an enormous index finger into his mouth; then, muttering under his curled and varnished moustache, he picked up an instrument from the table.

The show now began in earnest. Gripping the arms of the chair, des Esseintes felt a cold sensation on his cheek, thirty-six candles flashed before his eyes, the most hideous pains shot through him, he drummed his feet and bellowed like a beast in a slaughterhouse.

There was a cracking sound and part of the molar broke off; he felt as if his head was being wrenched from his shoulders, his skull shattered; he went mad, screaming at the top of his voice and furiously fighting off the man who rushed at him again as if he was trying to get his arm down into his stomach. Suddenly the man stepped back, lifted des Esseintes bodily into the air by his jaw, then brutally dropped him onto his backside in the chair, staggered upright, panting with effort, his frame blocking the window, and brandished the blue stump of a tooth, dripping with red, at the end of his pincers!

Annihilated, des Esseintes threw up a bowlful of blood, waved away the old woman's offer of the tooth wrapped in newspaper, paid two francs, and added his own bloody globules of spittle to the stairway before fleeing to the street; outside he felt suddenly joyful, ten years younger, and fascinated by the smallest thing...

J.K. Huysmans, *À Rebours*, IV.

CHAPTER 10

THE IMPOSSIBLE PUDDING

A pre-eminent, possibly unassailable, candidate for the title of Decadent Pâtissier of All Time is Marie-Antoine Carême (1784-1833). His masterpieces would probably have been too namby-pamby for De Sade - there's a noticeable lack of breasts, buttocks and genitalia in his repertoire - but he had other Decadent qualities. He was a mad perfectionist, theatrical, luxurious, obsessive and extreme. 'The fine arts,' he once wrote, 'are five in number: painting, sculpture, poetry, music, architecture - whose main branch is confectionery'.

His first job was as a kitchen assistant in a Paris restaurant. From there he graduated to Bailly's *pâtisserie* in the Rue Vivienne, spending his free time copying architectural drawings in the print-room of the *Bibliothèque nationale*. One of Bailly's customers was the Foreign Minister, Prince Talleyrand, who took on Carême as his chef, and was soon using his magnificent culinary talents to dazzle foreign ambassadors into acquiescence. After this spell as an unofficial arm of French diplomacy, Carême went on to direct the *service de bouche* of the Prince Regent of England (the future King George IV), Tsar Alexander I of Russia, the Emperor of Austria, the British Embassy in Paris, the Prince of Württemberg, the Marquess of Londonderry, Princess Bagration, and Baron de Rothschild. He specialized in fantastic sculptures of meringue, pastry, spun sugar and fruit, and the list of his *pièces montées* includes creations that would seem to belong more to the opera-house than the table: harps, lyres, globes, military helmets, trophies of war, pyramids, vases, a Chinese hermitage, an Indian pavilion, a waterfall with palm-trees, a rustic cottage, a Venetian gondola, the ruins of Palmyra, etc. After replicating almost the whole world in edible form, this temperamental and brilliant man died aged 50, 'burnt out by the flame of his genius and the charcoal of the roasting-spit.'

The following recipes, none of which should take more than 30 or 40 hours to prepare, are taken from *French Cookery: comprising L'Art de la Cuisine francaise; le Pâtissier royal; le Cuisinier parisien* , by the late M. Carême, some time Chef of the kitchen of His Majesty George IV, translated by William Hall, cook to T.P. Williams Esq., M.P., and conductor of the Parliamentary Dinners of the Right Honourable Lord Viscount Canterbury, G.C.B., late Speaker of the House of Commons (John Murray, London, 1836).

GROS MERINGUE À LA PARISIENNE

———•●•———

This is actually seven recipes in one. The finished article is a pastry globe coated in meringue, studded with miniature choux-buns and pistachios, and filled with macaroons, strawberries and whipped cream. It balances on three drum-shaped cakes of increasing diameter, each drum made up of several minor cakes, wafers, meringues, nougats and biscuits. It looks more like a monument to the Spirit of Enterprise than a pudding, and the calories it contains, if converted into an alternative form of energy, would have heated Napoleonic Paris for a weekend.

Before you start trying to create this colossal dish, prepare the necessary *pâte d'office, gaufres aux pistaches, petits pains à la Duchesse, meringues, petits choux, nougats,* and *croquignoles* . Carême's recipes for these are given after the main recipe.

———•●•———

Make three pounds of Pâte d'Office. Cut this paste in four portions, mould them, and roll them out of the thickness of one-sixth part of an inch. Lay one on a large baking sheet slightly buttered, cut it round twenty inches in diameter; lay another on a smaller sheet, cut it fifteen inches wide, and a third ten inches wide.

Cover with the remaining paste two moulds slightly buttered, each forming a dome, which, when united, compose a perfect globe eight inches in diameter. Cut the paste round, about one-fourth of an inch from the rim of the mould, prick the paste with the point of a knife that the air may escape; place them on baking-sheets.

Make yet another sheet, six inches wide, and the thickness of the others. Fold up the trimmings, and roll them in round bands half an inch thick, divide them in columns three inches long, lay them on a buttered baking-sheet.

Wash the four sheets over with egg, and prick them; put all

of them in an oven of a moderate heat, and when the domes begin to colour remove them from the oven, and turn the sheets that they may take an even colour. Then take them out, as also the supports when throughly dry.

Make forty pistachio wafers (see *Gaufres aux Pistaches**) three inches long by two and a half wide, and fold them over the gaufre-stick. Make also sixty *Pains à la Duchesse* * two inches long; let the *Gaufres* and *Pains* be of a light colour.

Trim the edges of the domes, and then with the point of a knife make an opening one inch wide in the centre of one of them; in the other an opening, also, two inches and a half wide.

Whip six whites of eggs very firm, and mix them with eight ounces of finely sifted sugar, as for *Meringues**; put half of this mixture over each dome, spread it with a knife (of an equal thickness), and throw fine sugar on it; set them in a mild oven, and give them a light colour.

Glaze the *Pains à la Duchesse* with caramel sugar; trim; and having wetted the edges of the boards with whites of egg, dip them in red or green chopped almonds, or in coloured sugar grains.

When the domes are thoroughly dry, whip six other whites of eggs, and mix eight ounces of sugar with them, as before, and form with the mixture thirty small *Meringues* one inch wide, and of the same height; mask them with sugar through a silk sieve, and when it is melted throw over them some sugar in grains, and put them in the oven directly, laid on a board.

Then make one ordinary-sized *Meringue*, round; finish it as the others, and place it beside them. Have half a pound of fine green pistachios (skinned), and each divided in two fillets only; then spread half the remaining white of egg, very even, over the dome, with the small hole, and strew fine sugar over it; this is to keep the pistachios fast, which stick upon it symmetrically, with the points upwards, leaving six straight places, on which the *Meringues* are afterwards to be placed (see the design). Strew sugar (in grains) over the pistachios only. Put it into a very slow oven. Dispose of the other dome in the same manner, but letting the points of the pistachios bend downwards.

When the *Meringues* are dried, and quit the paper easily, place three of them on the dome with the small hole, laying the first on the white part nearest the border; the second a quarter of

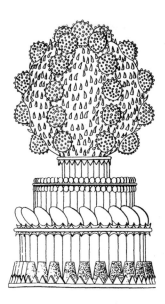

an inch above the first; the third the same distance from the second; range them on the five other spaces in the same manner. Replace them in the oven, and when equally coloured withdraw them; thus forming one single *Meringue*.

Range on the second dome six *Meringues* on the spaces between the pistachios, a quarter of an inch from the edge, and the other six the same distance above them; set them in the oven to colour.

Boil six ounces of sugar to a caramel, pour three-fourths of it onto a stewpan-cover lightly buttered, mask the fire in the stove with some ashes to deaden it, but yet to leave sufficient heat to keep the sugar in a syrup. Lay the largest board on a double sheet of paper, upon the back of a baking-sheet, put the washed side of the next in size downwards on the larger one. Dip a *Gaufre* at one end into the sugar, and stick it immediately on the smaller sheet, one-sixth of an inch from the edge; dip another, and stick close to the last, and so proceed all round, setting them upright, and at the same distance from the edge. Dip six of the supports at one end into the sugar, and place them upright on the edge of the baking-sheet on which the board is lying, that the caramel on them may spread out.

Warm the sugar remaining in the pan, and when melted, dip the other ends of the supports into it, and place them immediately in the centre of the board, two inches from each other. Whilst the sugar is hot, put a little on the ends of the supports arranged for that purpose, by the sugar already there; turn this stand over quickly on the centre of the larger sheet, pressing on it gently that the supports may adhere to it.

Form the other two steps in the same manner, with the *petits pains*, with coffee icing, and form a neat border of small white pastries round the edges of each stand. Garnish round the lower stand with small *nougats**; the second with *petits choux**, with chocolate icings, and filled with apricot jam. Stick them on slightly with a little caramel.

Then place the *Meringue*, with the largest opening, on the third sheet, giving it the appearance of a cup, and fixing eight macaroons, or *croquignoles**, round the bottom within it, partly to the sheet, and partly to the cup, to prevent it falling; as also eight more just within the upper edge of the cup, but rising above it sufficiently to prevent the upper dome from shaking off.

Lift (with one finger through the small hole) the second dome on the first, and on the hole fix the largest of the lesser *Meringues*. When serving, take off the upper dome, and fill the lower *Meringue* with the *Crème Chantilly*, seasoned with vanille, and lay on the cream (which should form a paramid) some strawberries; then fill with cream the small *Meringue* for the centre of the top of the large one, (as the design represents). The person whose office it is to serve the dish should raise the upper dome, and breaking it in pieces, should give a spoonful of cream, and on one side of it a fragment of the *Meringue*.

PÂTE D'OFFICE

(OFFICE, OR CONFECTIONER'S PASTE)

———•◦•———

Sift one pound and a half of flour, make a hollow in it, and put in two eggs and three yolks, one pound of pounded sugar, and a little salt; stir these for two minutes, that the sugar may be somewhat melted, then work in the flour, and if necessary, another yolk, so as to render it as firm as if for building a pie. *Fraisez* it five or six times by rubbing the mixture between the hands and the dresser until a sort of crumb, like bread-crumbs, is produced, which gradually moisten, mixing and rubbing it lightly till it becomes a mass; then work it by passing it in small pieces between the pressure of the hands and the dresser to mingle the soft and the hard parts together, forming it into one equally smooth and firm body... The paste should be firm, and yet soft enough to mould easily; otherwise add another yolk or white of egg.

Afterwards cut the paste in pieces, mould and roll it of the thickness of one-sixth of an inch, to serve for the bottoms (or boards) of a *pièce montée.* Put the paste on a baking-sheet lightly buttered, and with the fingers press out the air between the paste and the sheet (without this precaution the heat would deform it, and from the heat not acting equally throughout, it would possess less solidity). When thus arranged, cut it with the point of a knife, as may be wished, and prick it to assist the escape of air. Wash the surface lightly, but not the sides, put it into a moderate oven, and if it blisters, pass the blade of a large knife under it, and (if done enough) turn it over to obtain a light brown colour on both sides.

When taken from the oven lay it on the most even part of the dresser, and place the baking-sheet upon it to remain until cold, when the paste will be perfectly level on both sides.

All boards of Pâte d'Office are thus made: the preparation will succeed perfectly by using twelve ounces instead of one pound of sugar.

Gaufres aux Pistaches

(Pistachio Wafers)

———•◦•———

Skin and cut in fillets, as thin as possible, half a pound of sweet almonds, mix them with four ounces of pounded sugar, half a table-spoonful of flour, the rind of an orange grated, two whole eggs, and one yolk, and a pinch of salt; stir them gently, so as not to break the almonds; when well mixed, rub wax on a baking-sheet, eighteen inches long by twelve inches wide, on which spread the preparation very even, arranging the almonds with a fork; then strew two ounces of pistachios cut in fillets upon them, and put them into an oven of a moderate heat, until of a fine clear light brown colour, and the same underneath; cover them with paper, if they are not coloured at the bottom, to keep them light at top; watch for the exact moment when they are done, as a moment too much renders them too brittle to give them any correct form, and if a moment too little, they will not preserve their shape, and instead of being crisp, will be very disagreeable eating; when perfectly baked, cut them in pieces two inches square (or in lengths one inch and a half wide, and two inches and a half long), and keep the baking-sheet at the mouth of the oven, whilst you fold these squares over a round stick one inch and a half in diameter, and four or five feet long; as this operation must be performed whilst they are hot, it would be a better method to lay them on two baking-sheets, putting the second to bake four or five minutes after the first, thus obtaining time to perform it with more success and certainty. The preparation for these wafers may be made with five yolks, or five whites, without any detriment to the operation, and they may be served without folding them, by cutting them three inches in length, and one inch in width only; and dip the edges of them neatly into caramel sugar, and then into some chopped pistachios, so that the wafers are green all round; spread apple or white currant jelly on the bottom of one, and lay another on it; in this manner, *gaufres au gros sucre* are made; or the sugar may be mingled with two ounces of chopped pistachios, producing a fine effect, and easily accomplished.

Petits Pains à la Duchesse

(Small Loaves, the Duchess's Mode)

Put into a stewpan a pint of water, with two ounces of fresh butter; when boiling, remove it from the fire, and mix with it six ounces of sifted flour; work it smooth, and dry it for a few minutes as usual; change the stewpan, and add two eggs and two ounces of pounded sugar; the whole well mixed, add two eggs and the rind of a lemon chopped fine; then again add an egg or two, as the paste may require; it should be less rich in butter, eggs, or flour than any of the former described, as making more effect in the oven, it become hollow within, and is filled with creams or sweetmeats, as the following articles direct; sprinkle the dresser with flour, roll out the *choux* of the ordinary thickness, very equally, and three inches in length (use the least flour possible, that they may appear more clear when baked); place them on a baking-sheet, two inches apart, egg them slightly, and put them in an oven somewhat hotter than for the *choux* usually; when they are well dried, which is known by their being firm to the touch, glaze them with sugar through a sieve, and the salamander; take them from the baking-sheet immediately; when they are cold, open that at the side, and fill them with apricot, or peach jam, or currant jelly, close them and dish; the *choux glaces* are thus formed, but made less, and round.

Choux à la Mecque
(Mecca Choux)

Put into a stewpan a pint of milk and two ounces of fresh butter, make it into a soft paste with flour, dry it for a few minutes, and add two ounces of butter, and a gill of milk; dry it again; change the stewpan, and add two eggs and two ounces of pounded sugar; when well blended, add two more eggs, two spoonsful of whipt cream, and a grain of salt (the paste must not be softer than usual); arrange these *choux* with a spoon, in lengths of three inches; when they are egged, mask them with sugar in grains, and bake them in a moderate oven; serve them of a fine colour: they may be flavoured with citron, orange, or lemon, by rasping the half of the skin of either on sugar, and weighing it as part of the two ounces used in the preparation.

MERINGUES À LA BIGARADE

(MERINGUES FLAVOURED WITH SEVILLE ORANGE PEEL)

———•◦•———

Rasp on a lump of sugar the rind of a ripe yellow Seville orange, dry this sugar at the mouth of the oven, pound and sift it, add other sugar to make with this the weight of eight ounces; whip six whites of eggs in a basin, and when very firm add the sugar by a little at a time, stirring it into the whites with a whisk; when worked enough, which is perceptible by its separating easily from the spoon, in moulding the meringues, form them on strips of paper, disposed according to the size required; they are generally shaped like an egg cut in half, so that when two are joined, they should be of an egg shape; when they are moulded, throw sugar over them, not too finely pounded, and when the sugar has remained some minutes, blow off the overplus from them; take the paper by the two ends, and lay it on a small board, an inch thick; put them in a slow oven until of a fine red tint, and covered with small pearls; then raise them from the paper, and with a teaspoon press down the softer part in the inside; lay them again on a baking-sheet, with this side upwards, and replace them in the oven, until they take an even colour when cold: these meringues will keep for a month in a dry place: fill them with whipt cream seasoned with the rind of a Seville orange, but do not put the cream in until the instant they are going to table, as the cream softens them greatly; the cream may be flavoured with marasquin or any other flavour commonly used.

Nougats à la Francaise

(Nougat, French manner)

Skin three-quarters of a pound of filberts, separate each in two pieces, lay them on a baking-sheet in a slow oven, observe and turn them from time to time, that they may become of an even colour; when lightly browned, bring them to the mouth of the oven; boil six ounces of sugar to caramel, and the moment it is at the proper point, stir the kernels in gently with a wooden spoon (not to break them), covering them equally with the sugar; the nougat should be of a fine light-red tint, then turn it out upon a baking-sheet slightly buttered, spread it quickly, and strew upon it sugar in grains, and pistachios cut in fillets, and dried at the mouth of the oven; from the *nougat* eight inches long, and six inches wide, and, above all, of an equal thickness (do not handle it too much, lest you break the grained sugar); when sufficiently cold to resist the knife, yet not so cold as to cause it to fly in pieces, trim it round the edges, cut it in two equal lengths, and divide each into fifteen pieces of the same width; these *nougats* may be made with almonds, and garnished with currants, red or white aniseed, or sugar in grains.

Croquignoles à la Francaise

(French mode)

Perfectly crush eight ounces of bitter macaroons, and sift them, put them into eight ounces of flour and make a hollow in it, adding six ounces of sugar, three yolks of eggs, three ounces of fresh butter, and a grain of salt, work the whole together as usual; form the *croquignoles* of the size of an olive, and having slightly egged them, put them into a gentle oven to bake of a light brown colour; filbert macaroons, or sweet macaroons flavoured with the rind of cedrata, lemon, &c, or with vanille, candied orange flowers, or aniseed, may thus be used.

A FEW CRÈMES FOUETTÉES

These come from Carême too. They're much less daunting to prepare than the Gros Meringue, but still luxurious and possibly even more dangerous to the cardio-vascular system.

CRÈME FOUETTÉE AU MARASQUIN

Set a quart of double cream in a basin on pounded ice for two hours, mixing it with a pinch of gum tragacanth in powder; then whip it with a whisk for fifteen minutes, when the cream should be light and stiff; when perfectly drained (upon a sieve) mix it in a basin with six ounces of pounded sugar: the whole well-mingled, and at the moment of serving add the third part of a half pint of marasquin; serve the cream in a crust of tart paste, or a *vol-au-vent* glazed with a sultan over it, or in almond paste cups, a silver stewpan, or bowl; rum may be thus employed.

CRÈME FOUETTÉE AU CHOCOLAT

Melt four ounces of chocolate in a teacupful of boiling water; when cold mix it with the cream with four ounces of pounded sugar.

CRÈME FOUETTÉE À LA VANILLE

Chop half a stick of good vanille very fine, pound it with two ounces of sugar and sift it through a silk sieve, add four ounces of pounded sugar to it, and with it flavour the whipt cream as above.

Crème fouettée à la Fleur d'Orange pralinée

Pound half an ounce of candied orange-flowers, which mix with six ounces of pounded sugar in the whipt cream as directed; or the cream may be seasoned with a spoonful of double orange-flower water.

Crème fouettée à la Rose

The cream being whipt as usual, mingle it with half a spoonful of essence of roses, six ounces of pounded sugar, and a slight infusion of cochineal, carmine, or *rouge végétal*; but it may be served without; if served white, some large fine strawberries may be placed upon it.

L'Anglais décrit dans le château fermé

by André Pieyre de Mandiargues

The shit was very tasty. I helped myself to as much of it as I had the fish sperm. I would have taken more if the negroes hadn't carried it away. The next dish to arrive was stuffed cow's vulva, so I was informed. From the gastronomic point of view, they were full of the most refined ingredients imaginable. Very white in colour and plump, they floated in a bone marrow sauce like little inflatable boats. To accompany them, we had giant asparagus. These Edmonde served to us one at a time with mock prudishness. Having consumed all that, the black waiters returned from the kitchen with two dishes of seabird brains. At first sight I was rather taken aback by their curious arrangement; for each brain, somewhere in size between a hazelnut and a walnut, had been stuck onto a beak. The idea was to pick up the little skull (which had been thoroughly cleaned), raise it to your lips and pull off the mouthful of brain which was crisp on the outside and a little raw in the middle.

"Go ahead, eat!" said Montcul, surprised by my reluctance. "They're exceedingly rich in phosphorus, you know".

I ignored his advice, however. The brains had an after-taste of fish oil which put me off. And then I began thinking, not without a certain unease, about the bloodbath this dish must have entailed — several hundred seagulls killed for just two plates! And yet, why hadn't I considered that it must have required slaughter on a similar scale to provide one dish of vulvas? The reason, no doubt, was because I found the vulvas delicious, whereas the brains were disgusting. This opinion was not shared by the negroes. They polished off both plates of brains avidly.

When the dishes of seabird brains had been removed, Viola stuck her tongue out in such a way that made my balls tingle and informed me that dessert was about to appear. I assumed this meant fruit, gateaux and such like, but when I saw Gracchus and Publicola enter, staggering under the weight of an enormous dish, I wondered if I hadn't become drunk without realising it, or perhaps I was having some sort of mystical hallucination. Their dish was piled high with lobster, langoustine, crab and prawns. At moments it looked as if they were about to drop the lot (if this was just play-acting, we were certainly taken in by it) but finally they succeeded in placing it on the table. Nothing could have provided a more elaborate adornment for the silver table than this monstrous prickly bush made up of claws, humps, antennae and spikes. However, an even greater delight awaited us. The chef had removed the salty meat from these crustaceans and replaced it with confectionery. So, when we tore off a limb or cracked open a shell, we found inside creme bavaroise, citron and rose jam, chestnut puree, walnut, vanilla and chocolate paste, praline or coffee fondant, pistachio marzipan and sugar flowers. The pleasures of the palate were mixed with the delight of unexpected and heedless destruction. After a while (during which time I had consumed the contents of a small lobster, an edible crab, two velvet swimming crabs and a handful of prawns) the serving dish was almost empty. Nobody spoke during this course, except to announce, like in a card game, what we had in our hand. It was a veritable feast — but then, the voice of our host returned us to other matters.

"Edmonde", he stated, "If I were you I'd be stuffing myself less and thinking more about my arsehole. No matter that you have been put to the test by Caligula's weapon and every other cock that's visited this chateau! I tell you, taking a great prick made of ice in the arse is another matter. It's been known to split a person's guts."

"Oh please no, anything but that!" she begged. "Punish me any way you wish, if you think I ought to be punished. Let me be buggered by everyone here, even the women, with those dreadful dildoes of yours. Have me beaten. Bring in the dog. Anything you want, but spare me the ice."

"You will be spared nothing. Have the great penis brought in immediately."

While Gracchus went out to the refrigerator, our host turned to me and said:

"My dearest Balthasar, you will carry out this operation. The honour is yours as it's your first evening at Gamehuche. But above all, do not let this whore off lightly. I'll be most put out if you do.

I was exaggerating just now when I said she was almost indispensible. There is nobody here who couldn't be replaced from one day to the next, if that's our pleasure."

It was a most gentlemanly offer, and I'd have liked to thank him in a similar fashion, but Gracchus had already returned with the great prick. My words were interrupted by cries of joy when this object appeared. It was lying in a long vessel lined with seal skin. This vessel in turn had been placed in a dish of crushed ice so there would be no reduction in its size during preparations for its use. Wearing woollen gloves, I took hold of the prick by the balls and felt the weight of it in my hands. It felt like one of those wild west Colts which could shatter an alligator's eye as effectively as a rifle. Viola lent me a little tape measure which, no doubt for shameless reasons, she kept in her stocking. With this I measured the implement before returning it to its cold store. Thirty nine centimetres long, with a diameter of twenty four centimetres in the middle and twenty five at the glans! Its dimensions made it a formidable weapon.

Meanwhile, Edmonde, realising that tears were to no avail, handed herself over to our black waiters in preparation for the sacrifice.

From *L'Anglais décrit dans le château fermé*
by André Pieyre de Mandiargues.

André Pieyre de Mandiargues (1909-1991) was a prolific storyteller, novelist and art critic. Most of his work, including *L'Anglais décrit dans le château fermé*, has yet to be translated into English. His short stories 'Clorinde' and 'Moon Walker' are included in Michael Richardson's two volume study of surrealism - *The Dedalus Book of Surrealism* (1993) and *The Myth of the World: Surrealism 2* (1994).

CHAPTER 11

ANGELS AND DEVILS

Throughout *À Rebours*, the handbook of Decadence, the hero des Esseintes spends much time and effort exploring the more outlandish areas of experience and creating a new and artificial world out of his nervous sensibility. His customized aesthete's paradise in Fontenay-aux-Roses is a hothouse full of rare flowers and scents, luxurious materials and precious stones, 'a comfortable desert' where he can take refuge 'far from the interminable deluge of human stupidity'. But the world he creates lacks durability. His pleasures are all short-lived, his health breaks down, he can never find contentment or peace. The book ends with a kind of *de profundis*, a forlorn plea that this arch-aesthete might rediscover faith and hope.

The author's personal odyssey took a similar turn. Huysmans was a civil servant, working in the Ministry of the Interior in Paris, compiling surveillance reports for the Sûreté on anarchists, political subversives, unwanted foreigners and illegal gambling clubs. He was a pillar of social hygiene, a modern bureaucrat-Inquisitor. In his private life, though, he was just the opposite: obsessed with all the things it was his job to keep a check on, he dabbled in satanism, spiritism and other occult practices, as well as enjoying straight, weird, casual and demonic sex. He never married, and preferred emotional independence. 'In the end,' he wrote in one weary letter, 'there's nothing real but the brothel. At least it's all over when you come out.' As he grew older, the weariness intensified, his health failed, and he turned his back on a sinful past. Never one for half-measures, he became a lay member of an order of Trappist monks.

Barbey d'Aurevilly predicted Huysmans' conversion ten years before it happened. Reviewing *A Rebours* he wrote, 'After a book like this, the author has only two choices: the muzzle of a pistol or the foot of the Cross.'

This is a familiar dilemma for Decadents, who never walk quite as blithely into hell as they would like, and often have secret hopes of redemption. But whose side are they really on - the angels

or the devils? Huysmans was painfully divided. So was his
admirer Oscar Wilde, who managed to be both irreverent and
deeply religious at the same time. For Baudelaire it didn't seem to
matter which side you ended up on. The important thing was
simply to *go* - one way or the other. His poem *Le Voyage* ends with
the following words:

> *O Mort, vieux capitaine, il est temps! levons l'ancre!*
> *Ce pays nous ennuie, ô Mort! Appareillons!*
> *Si le ciel et la mer sont noirs comme de l'encre,*
> *Nos coeurs que tu connais sont remplis de rayons!*
>
> *Verse-nous ton poison pour qu'il nous réconforte!*
> *Nous voulons, tant ce feu nous brûle le cerveau,*
> *Plonger au fond du gouffre, Enfer ou Ciel, qu'importe?*
> *Au fond de l'Inconnu pour trouver du nouveau!*

> (Death, old captain, the time has come! Let's weigh
> anchor! This country's tedious, Death. Let's set sail.
> If the sky and the sea are as black as ink, our hearts,
> which you know so well, are filled with light.
>
> Pour out a dose of your poison for our comfort!
> There's such a fire burning in our heads that we
> long to throw ourselves into the abyss - Heaven or
> Hell, who cares? - into the unknown in
> search of the *new* !)

When it comes to cooking, Heaven and Hell of course each have their own traditions. Angels, we are told, eat manna - although this was contradicted by a mayor of Naples in the 1930s, the Duke of Bovino, who was convinced that the angels in Paradise eat nothing but *vermicelli al pomidoro*. Either way, it tends to confirm one's suspicions about the monotony of Paradise in general and the life of an angel in particular.

Information on what devils eat is more sketchy, although judging by images from Hieronymus Bosch and others, they probably snacked on slices of the damned. In fact Hell itself is often pictured as a gigantic kitchen, with roaring flames, spits, cauldrons, toasting forks, gridirons, etc. - all briskly cooking the carcasses of sinners while grinning fiends look on and prod them from time to time to see if they are done.

Looking at the choice of recipes from the two sides, it seems that, just as the Devil has all the best tunes, he probably comes off better in the kitchen as well. Devilled sauces are piquant, exciting, hot. Nothing as racy is attributed to Heaven. As Dr Kitchiner has it: 'Every man must have experienced that, when he has got deep into his third bottle, his palate acquires a degree of torpidity and his stomach is seized with a certain craving which seems to demand a stimulant to the powers of both. The provocatives used on such an occasion an ungrateful world has combined to term devils'.

DEVILLED PEPPERS

<hr>

6 LARGE RED PEPPERS

A SMALL GLASS OF OLIVE OIL

1 LEMON

FRESH BASIL

Grill the peppers until the skins turn black. This can be done under a hot grill, or else in a direct flame. Either way the peppers have to be turned regularly. It is important to keep the peppers whole so that any juice remains inside. When the skins have blackened, they can be peeled off very easily. Slice the peppers lengthways, taking care to retain any juice. Remove all the seeds and pith, then slice them into strips. Put the strips on a plate or shallow dish and sprinkle the olive oil, pepper juice and a little lemon juice over them. Chop some fresh basil and scatter that over the top. Leave the peppers in a cool place (not the fridge) over night and serve as an hors d'oeuvres the following day.

DEVILLED HAM TOASTS

<hr>

2 OZ LEAN COOKED HAM, FINELY MINCED

2 TEASPOONS OF WORCESTER SAUCE

A PINCH OF CAYENNE PEPPER

$^1/_2$ TABLESPOON OF FRENCH MUSTARD

$^1/_2$ OZ BUTTER

4 CIRCLES OF WELL-BUTTERED TOAST 2 INCHES IN DIAMETER

1 TABLESPOON FINELY CHOPPED PARSLEY

Thoroughly mix the ham, Worcester sauce, cayenne and mustard. Melt the butter in a small saucepan and stir the mixture into it. Keep stirring until it is very hot. Pile on to the circles of toast, sprinkle with parsley and serve immediately.

MEPHISTOPHELIAN SAUCE

(FOR TURKEY REMAINS)

Cut up the remains of the bird and rub with mustard. Sprinkle it with a little salt and a lot of cayenne pepper. Chop six shallots and put them in a stewpan with one and a half wine glasses of chilli vinegar, a chopped clove of garlic, two bay leaves and one ounce of glaze. Boil altogether for ten minutes. Add four tablespoons of tomato sauce, a little sugar and ten of gravy or brown sauce. Boil a few minutes longer then add a pat of butter. Pour over the heated turkey and serve.

ANGEL'S HAIR

CABELLOS DE ANGEL

So named because it is made with the fibrous part of a large ripe pumpkin, preferably kept from the previous season.

For 2kg of jam:

2 LB OF PUMPKIN OR SQUASH FIBRES.

2 LB OF SUGAR

$1^3/4$ PINTS OF WATER

1 LEMON

2 STICKS OF CINNAMON

You will need a pumpkin of about 2 kg in weight. Peel it and cut it into chunks. Put them into a large saucepan, and boil until it is quite soft. This should take about 20 minutes. Drain it and when cool enough to handle, remove the seeds, separate the fibres and drain it again thoroughly. Put aside 1 kg of the pumpkin fibre. Slice the lemon and add, together with the cinamon sticks and sugar, to the litre of water. This should be simmered until it forms a syrup.

At this point, remove the lemon and cinnamon and add the pumpkin fibres. Cook this slowly for an hour giving it an occasional stir. You can test if the angel's hair has reached the right consistency by putting a few drops on a cold plate. Tilt the plate and if the jam does not run, it is ready. Put into jars and seal.

ANGELS ON HORSEBACK

SIX FINGERS OF BREAD

2 OZ BUTTER

6 OYSTERS

3 RASHERS OF STREAKY BACON

LEMON JUICE

CAYENNE PEPPER

Fry the bread lightly in the butter and keep hot. Trim the beards from the oysters, sprinkle with lemon juice and cayenne and roll each one in half a rasher of streaky bacon. Fry quickly and carefully in butter for about two minutes. Make sure that the rolls are turned so that the bacon cooks on all sides. It will protect the oyster from being overcooked. Place a roll on each piece of fried bread and serve immediately.

If there's one creature in which Heaven and Hell seem to do battle, it's the monkfish, which is as ugly as sin but tastes divine. This may be why it's known as both the angel fish and the devil fish; it makes an ideal dish, of course, for the Decadent. Here are three ways of preparing it.

Buried and Roasted Venetian Monkfish

4 MONKFISH TAILS, SKINNED, CLEANED AND TRIMMED

8 LARGE POTATOES

BUTTER

OLIVE OIL

ROSEMARY

PARMESAN CHEESE

Slice the potatoes lengthwise as thinly as you can. Oil the bottom of a roasting pan, then cover it with a third of the potatoes, oiling and buttering between the layers. Put the monkfish on top, bury it in the rest of the potatoes, and sprinkle with oil, butter, rosemary, salt and pepper. Roast in a hot oven for one and a half to two hours, basting from time to time. Add grated Parmesan 10 minutes before the end.

Flaming Monk

A recipe adapted from Marinetti's *Cucina Futurista*, where it's called *Boccone Squadrista* (Blackshirt's Snack). Marinetti's book was designed to startle Italians out of their sleepy pasta-loving ways and fill them with ardour for war. Hopeless of course for that purpose, the book remains a handy source of culinary shock tactics.

4 FILLETS OF MONKFISH

2-3 LARGE APPLES

BUTTER

RUM

Bake each piece of fish between 2 large buttered slices of apple. Douse with rum, set on fire, and serve in flames.

MONKFISH CARDINAL

2 LB TOMATOES, SKINNED AND CHOPPED

1 ONION, CHOPPED FINELY

BUTTER

OLIVE OIL

BOUQUET GARNI

GARLIC

4 CLEANED MONKFISH TAILS

First make a tomato fondue. You do this by frying the onion gently in olive oil and butter until it is transparent and tender, then adding the tomatoes, salt, pepper, bouquet garni, and a clove of garlic crushed. Cover and cook until the tomatoes are reduced to a pulp. Uncover, stir and cook the mixture till it thickens. Then sieve and add a tablespoon of finely chopped parsley or other fresh herbs of your choice.

After that, place your monkfish in a roasting tin with some oil, salt and pepper, and bake it in a very hot oven (475 F, 240 C, Gas 9) for 10 minutes. Lower the heat to just plain hot (400 F, 200 C, Gas 6) and baste the fish occasionally until it's cooked: about 20-25 minutes.

Serve with the cardinal's cloak of tomato fondue laid out to one side, and garnish with grapes and mushrooms. Glasses of Chartreuse or Benedictine, Gregorian chants, nuns' or monks' habits, etc, will all add to the solemnity of the occasion.

HIMMEL UND ERDE
(HEAVEN AND EARTH)

Another theologically ambivalent dish. Despite the grandiose title, the ingredients are humble, the taste both earthy and sublime. (This recipe will feed three to four.)

2 LB OF POTATOES

2 LB OF APPLES

SALT

9 OZ STREAKY BACON

Peel the potatoes and quarter them. (If you are using new potatoes, they will need no more than cleaning.) Put them into a large pan of water and bring to the boil. Peel and quarter the apples. Allow the potatoes to boil for about 10 minutes before adding the apples. When the potatoes are cooked, the apples should be soft without falling apart.

Dice the bacon and fry it in a pan. The thicker the bacon the better and ideally it should have enough fat that you do not need to add any to the pan. When the bacon is crispy, drain the apples and potatoes and put them into a hot serving dish. Sprinkle the bacon plus juices on top and serve immediately.

All cooks need a rest from time to time, so for dessert we suggest something ready-made: not Angel Delight, because the taste hardly seems worth the effort of opening the packet, but a selection of French pastries, preferably from the Saint-Sulpice area of Paris, where the pâtissiers are outnumbered only by the ecclesiastical outfitters. Suitable items are *religieuses*, *nonnettes*, *jésuites*, *sacristains*, *oublies* and *pets de nonne* (or, more politely, *soupirs de nonne*). Follow or precede with Trappiste and Saint-Nectaire cheese, and accompany the meal with beer from the Abbey of Chimay, monastic liqueurs (Aiguebelle, Bénédictine, etc), or that old favourite, a bottle of Blue Nun.

VATHEK

by William Beckford

Prayer at break of day was announced, when Carathis and Vathek
ascended the steps, which led to the summit of the tower; where
they remained for some time though the weather was lowering
and wet. This impending gloom corresponded with their
malignant dispositions; but when the sun began to break through
the clouds, they ordered a pavilion to be raised, as a screen against
the intrusion of his beams. The Caliph, overcome with fatigue,
sought refreshment from repose; at the same time, hoping that
significant dreams might attend on his slumbers; whilst the
indefatigable Carathis, followed by a party of her mutes,
descended to prepare whatever she judged proper, for the oblation
of the approaching night.

By secret stairs, contrived within the thickness of the wall,
and known only to herself and her son, she first repaired to the
mysterious recesses in which were deposited the mummies that
had been wrested from the catacombs of the ancient Pharoahs. Of
these she ordered several to be taken. From thence, she resorted to
a gallery; where, under the guard of fifty female negroes mute and
blind of the right eye, were preserved the oil of the most venomous
serpents; rhinoceros' horns; and woods of a subtle and penetrating
odour, procured from the interior of the Indies, together with a
thousand other horrible rarities. This collection had been formed
for a purpose like the present, by Carathis herself; from a
presentiment, that she might one day, enjoy some intercourse with
the infernal powers: to whom she had ever been passionately
attached, and to whose taste she was no danger.

To familiarise herself the better with the horrors in view, the
Princess remained in the company of her negresses, who squinted
in the most amiable manner from the only eye they had; and leered
with exquisite delight, at the sculls and skeletons which Carathis
had drawn forth from her cabinets; all of them making the most
frightful contortions and uttering such shrill chatterings, that the
Princess stunned by them and suffocated by the potency of the

exhalations, was forced to quit the gallery, after stripping it of a part of its abominable treasures.

Whilst she was thus occupied, the Caliph, who instead of the visions he expected, had acquired in these unsubstantial regions a voracious appetite, was greatly provoked at the mutes, for having totally forgotten their deafness, he had impatiently asked them for food; and seeing them regardless of his demand, he began to cuff, pinch, and bite them, till Carathis arrived to terminate a scene so indecent, to the great content of these miserable creatures: "Son! what means all this?" said she, panting for breath. "I thought I heard as I came up, the shrieks of a thousand bats, torn from their crannies in the recesses of a cavern; and it was the outcry only of these poor mutes, whom you were so unmercifully abusing. In truth, you but ill deserve the admirable provision I have brought you." - "Give it me instantly," exclaimed the Caliph; "I am perishing for hunger!" - "As to that," answered she, "you must have an excellent stomach if it can digest what I have brought." - "Be quick," replied the Caliph; - "but, oh heavens! what horrors! what do you intend?" "Come; come;" returned Carathis, "be not so squeamish; but help me to arrange every thing properly; and you shall see that, what you reject with such symptoms of disgust, will soon complete your felicity. Let us get ready the pile, for the sacrifice of tonight; and think not of eating, till that is performed: know you not, that all solemn rites ought to be preceded by a rigorous abstinence?"

The Caliph, not daring to object, abandoned himself to grief and the wind that ravaged his entrails, whilst his mother went forward with the requisite operations. Phials of serpents' oil, mummies and bones, were soon set in order on the balustrade of the tower. The pile began to rise; and in three hours was twenty cubits high. At length darkness approached, and Carathis, having stripped herself to her inmost garment, clapped her hands in an impulse of ecstacy; the mutes followed her example; but Vathek, extenuated with hunger and impatience, was unable to support himself, and fell down in a swoon. The sparks had already kindled the dry wood; the venomous oil burst into a thousand blue flames; the mummies, dissolving, emitted a thick dun vapour; and the rhinoceros' horns, beginning to consume; all together diffused such a stench, that the Caliph, recovering, started from his trance, and gazed wildly on the scene in full blaze around him. The oil gushed forth in a plenitude of streams; and the negresses, who supplied it without intermission, united their cries to those of the Princess. At last, the fire became so violent, and the flames reflected from the polished marble so dazzling, that the Caliph, unable to withstand the heat and the blaze, effected his escape; and took shelter under the imperial standard.

In the mean time, the inhabitants of Samarah, scared at the light which shone over the city, arose in haste; ascended their roofs; beheld the tower on fire, and hurried, half naked to the square. Their love for their sovereign immediately awoke; and, apprehending him in danger of perishing in his tower, their whole thoughts were occupied with the means of his safety. Morakanabad flew from his retirement, wiped away his tears, and cried out for water like the rest. Bababalouk, whose olfactory nerves were more familiarized to magical odours, readily conjecturing, that Carathis was engaged in her favourite amusements, strenuously exhorted them not to be alarmed. Him, however, they treated as an old poltroon, and styled him a rascally traitor. The camels and dromedaries were advancing with water; but, no one knew by which way to enter the tower. Whilst the populace was obstinate in forcing the doors, a violent north-east wind drove an immense volume of flame against them. At first, they recoiled, but soon came back with redoubled zeal. At the same time, the stench of the horns and mummies increasing, most of the crowd fell backward in a state of suffocation. Those that kept their feet, mutually wondered at the cause of the smell; and admonished each other to retire. Morakanabad, more sick than the rest, remained in a piteous condition. Holding his nose with one hand, every one persisted in his efforts with the other to burst open the doors and obtain admission. A hundred and forty of the strongest and most resolute, at length accomplished their purpose. Having gained the stair-case, by their violent exertions, they attained a great height in a quarter of a hour.

Carathis, alarmed at the signs of her mutes, advanced to the stair-case; went down a few steps, and heard several voices calling out from below; "You shall, in a moment have water!" Being rather alert, considering her age, she presently regained the top of the tower; and bade her son suspend the sacrifice for some minutes; adding, - "We shall soon be enabled to render it more grateful. Certain dolts of your subjects, imagining no doubt that we were on fire, have been rash enough to break through those doors, which had hitherto remained inviolate; for the sake of bringing up water. They are very kind, you must allow, so soon to forget the wrongs you have done them; but that is of little moment. Let us offer them to the Giaour, - let them come up; our mutes, who neither want strength nor experience, will soon dispatch them; exhausted as they are, with fatigue." - "Be it so," answered the Caliph, "provided we finish, and I dine." In fact, these good people, out of breath from ascending fifteen hundred stairs in such haste; and chagrined, at having spilt by the way, the water they had taken, were no sooner arrived at the top, than the blaze of the flames, and the fumes of the mummies, at once overpowered their senses. It was a pity! for they beheld not the agreeable smile, with which the mutes and negresses adjusted the cord to their necks; these amiable personages rejoiced, however, no less at the scene. Never before had the ceremony of strangling been performed with so much facility. They all fell, without the least resistance or struggle: so that Vathek, in the space of a few moments, found himself surrounded by the dead bodies of the most faithful of his subjects; all which were thrown on the top of the pile. Carathis, whose presence of mind never forsook her, perceiving that she had carcasses sufficient to complete her oblation, commanded the chains to be stretched across the stair-case, and the iron doors barricaded, that no more might come up.

No sooner were these orders obeyed, than the tower shook; the dead bodies vanished in the flames; which, at once, changed from a swarthy crimson, to a bright rose colour: an ambient vapour emitted the most exquisite fragrance; the marble columns rang with harmonious sounds, and the liquified horns diffused a delicious perfume. Carathis, in transports, anticipated the success of her enterprise; whilst her mutes and negresses, to whom these sweets had given the cholic, retired grumbling to their cells.

Scarcely were they gone, when, instead of the pile, horns, mummies and ashes, the Caliph both saw and felt, with a degree of pleasure which he could not express, a table, covered with the most magnificent repast: availed himself, without scruple, of such an entertainment; and had already laid hands on a lamb stuffed with pistachios, whilst Carathis was privately drawing from a fillagreen urn, a parchment that seemed to be endless; and which had escaped the notice of her son. Totally occupied in gratifying an importunate appetite, he left her to peruse it without interruption; which having finished, she said to him, in an authoritative tone, "Put an end to your gluttony, and hear the splendid promises with which you are favoured!" She then read, as follows: "Vathek, my well-beloved, thou has surpassed my hopes: my nostrils have been regaled by the savour of thy mummies, thy horns; and, still more by the lives, devoted on the pile. At the full of the moon, cause the bands of thy musicians, and thy tymbals, to be heard; depart from thy palace, surrounded by all the pageants of majesty; thy most faithful slaves, thy best beloved wives; thy most magnificent litters; thy richest loaden camels; and set forward on thy way to Istakhar. There, I await thy coming: that is the region of wonders: there shalt thou receive the diadem of Gian Ben Gian; the talismans of Soliman; and the treasures of the pre-adamite sultans: there shalt thou be solaced with all kinds of delight. - But, beware how thou enterest any dwelling on thy route; or thou shalt feel the effects of my anger."

The Caliph, notwithstanding his habitual luxury, had never before dined with so much satisfaction. He gave full scope to the joy of these golden tidings; and betook himself to drinking anew. Carathis, whose antipathy to wine was by no means insuperable, failed not to pledge him at every bumper he ironically quaffed to the health of Mahomet. This infernal liquor completed their impious temerity, and prompted them to utter a profusion of blasphemies. They gave a loose to their wit, at the expense of the ass of Balaam, the dog of the seven sleepers, and the other animals admitted into the paradise of Mahomet. In this sprightly humour, they descended the fifteen hundred stairs, diverting themselves as they went, at the anxious faces they saw on the square, through the barbacans and loop-holes of the tower; and, at length, arrived at the royal apartments, by the subterranean passage. Bababalouk was parading to and fro, and issuing his mandates, with great pomp to the eunuchs; who were snuffing the lights and painting the eyes of the Circassians. No sooner did he catch sight of the Caliph and his mother, than he exclaimed, "Hah! you have, then, I perceive, escaped from the flames: I was not, however, altogether out of doubt." - "Of what moment is it to us what you thought, or think?" cried Carathis: "go; speed; tell Morakanabad that we immediately want him: and take care, not to stop by the way, to make you insipid reflections."

Morakanabad delayed not to obey the summons; and was received by Vathek and his mother, with great solemnity. They told him, with an air of composure and commiseration, that the fire at the top of the tower was extinguished; but that it had cost the lives of the brave people who sought to assist them.

"Still more misfortunes!" cried Morakanabad, with a sigh. "Ah, commander of the faithful, our holy prophet is certainly irritated against us! it behoves you to appease him." - "You will have leisure sufficient for your supplications, during my absence: for this country is the bane of my health. I am disgusted with the mountain of the four fountains, and am resolved to go and drink of the stream of Rocnabad. I long to refresh myself, in the delightful vallies which it waters. Do you, with the advice of my mother, govern my dominions, and take care to supply whatever her experiments may demand: for, you well know, that our tower abounds in materials for the advancement of science."

The tower but ill-suited Morakanabad's taste. Immense treasures had been lavished upon it; and nothing had he ever seen carried thither but female negroes, mutes and abominable drugs. Nor did he know well what to think of Carathis, who, like a cameleon, could assume all possible colours. Her cursed eloquence had often driven the poor mussulman to his last shifts. He considered, however, that if she possessed but few good qualities, her son had still fewer; and that the alternative, on the whole, would be in her favour. Consoled, therefore, with this reflection; he went, in good spirits, to soothe the populace, and make the proper arrangements for his master's journey.

William Beckford, *Vathek.*

CHAPTER 12

POSTSCRIPT

AMBLONGUS IN CALABRIA

Decadence begins with world-weariness, ennui, weltschmerz. It usually ends in madness, damnation, or a desolate return to the confessional. But even before the final crisis, a contradiction is reached: no matter how exotic or exquisite an experience might be, it always becomes dull with repetition. So the Decadent pushes on, trying new, ever-riskier sensations. Then these grow stale too. He becomes a kind of Sisyphus, heaving the boulder of his boredom up the long mountain-slope of experiment, only to have it crash to the bottom again the moment he reaches the peak.

So, after you've tasted the most bizarre and the rarest dish, what next? The answer in Huysmans' eyes was to turn to the spiritual - fasting, mortification and prayer. D'Annunzio, like Baudelaire, thought he might find it - the ultimate, unique, unrepeatable experience - in death. But these solutions are too grim. A third way seems more appealing. It was sketched out by that great Victorian painter, traveller and master of tomfoolery, Edward Lear.

In August 1847, Lear was travelling around the region of Calabria, Southern Italy. On the fourth of that month he found himself in the small town of Staiti. There he had been recommended to one Don Domenico Musitani, 'the chief man of the place'. Lear writes:

'Life in these regions of natural magnificence is full of vivid contrasts. The golden abstract vision of the hanging woods and crags were suddenly opposed to the realities of Don D. Musitani's rooms, which were so full of silkworms as to be beyond measure disgusting. To the cultivation of this domestic creature all Staiti is devoted; yellow cocoons in immense heaps are piled up in every possible place, and the atmosphere has to be conceived rather than described.'

The following day, Lear and his companion set out to do some sightseeing and sketching in the area.

'Staiti has its full share of Calabrian mystery in its buildings, caves and rocks, and employed our pencils far and near till noon, when we returned to our hosts to find dinner laid out in one of the bedrooms, all among the silkworms as before. Nor did the annoyance of a small tribe of spoiled children and barking dogs add charms to the meal.

But the 'vermi di seti' were our chief horror; and so completely did silkworms seem the life and air, end and material, of all Staiti, that we felt more than half sure, on contemplating three or four suspicious-looking dishes, that those interesting lepidoptera fomed a great part of the ground work of our banquet - silkworms (plain boiled), stewed chrysalis and moth tart!'

Later in the same month of August, Lear had moved on to the town of Stignano, which he describes as 'oppressive'. There he found lodgings with a rather intimidating family called Caristo. During the course of his stay, however, he was inadvertently presented with a dish which seems to have quite taken his fancy.

'... the most remarkable accident during our stay was caused by a small juvenile Caristo who, during the mid-day meal, climbed abruptly on to the table, and before he could be rescued, performed a series of struggles among the dishes, which ended by the little pickle's losing his balance and collapsing into the very middle of the macaroni dish! ...

One sees in Valentines, Cupids on beds of roses, or on birds' nests. But a slightly clothed Calabrese infant sitting in the midst of a hot dish of macaroni appears to me a perfectly novel idea!'

Among Lear's uncollected prose pieces is the following, dated September 1859.

'For a long time I fed on an immense leg of mutton - far, far larger than any leg of mutton I ever saw before or since.

But one day, I remembered that I had gone to the window to see a Circus Company go by, and attached to that there was an elephant. And I then had the horrid recollection that the Circus had long since returned (I saw it pass by) but the elephant never had.

From that moment I felt what that large leg of preposterous mutton really was, e non mangiar avante *- and I did not eat any more!*

On the whole I do not recommend dead elephant as daily food!'

Nonsense has been defined as 'Decadence under the sign of the comic'. If that's the case, surely some of the most decadent dishes ever conceived are the recipes in Lear's *Book of Nonsense*. Here they are.

AMBLONGUS PIE

Take 4 pounds (say 4 1/2 pounds) of fresh Amblonguses, and put them into a small pipkin.

Cover them with water and boil them for 8 hours incessantly, after which add 2 pints of new milk and proceed to boil for 4 hours more.

When you have ascertained that the Amblonguses are quite soft, take them out and place them in a wide pan, taking care to shake them well previously.

Grate some nutmeg over the surface and cover them carefully with powdered gingerbread, curry powder, and a sufficient quantity of Cayenne pepper.

Remove the pan into the next room and place it on the floor. Bring it back again and let it simmer for three-quarters of an hour. Shake the pan violently till all the Amblonguses have become of a pale purple colour.

Then, having prepared the paste, insert the whole carefully adding at the same time a small pigeon, 2 slices of beef, 4 cauliflowers and any number of oysters.

Watch patiently till the crust begins to rise and add a pinch of salt from time to time.

Serve up in a clean dish, and throw the whole out of the window as fast as possible.

If you found that particular recipe to your taste, then why not try these two from the same volume:

CRUMBOBBLIOUS CUTLETS

Procure some strips of beef and having cut them into the smallest possible slices, proceed to cut them still smaller, eight or perhaps nine times.

When the whole is thus minced, brush it up hastily with a new clothes-brush, and stir round rapidly and capriciously with a salt-spoon or a soup-ladle.

Place the whole in a saucepan, and remove it to a sunny place, - say the roof of the house if free from sparrows and other birds, - and leave it there for about a week.

At the end of that time add a little lavender, some oil of almonds, and a few herring-bones; and then cover the whole with 4 gallons of clarified crumbobblious sauce, when it will be ready for use.

Cut it into the shape of ordinary cutlets, and serve up in a clean tablecloth or dinner-napkin.

GOSKY PATTIES

Take a pig, three or four years of age, and tie him by the off hind leg to a post. Place 5 pounds of currants, 3 of sugar, 2 pecks of peas, 18 roast chestnuts, a candle, and 6 bushels of turnips within his reach; if he eats these, constantly provide him with more.

Then procure some cream, some slices of Cheshire cheese, four quires of foolscap paper and a packet of black pins. Work the whole into a paste, and spread it out to dry on a sheet of clean brown waterproof linen. When the paste is perfectly dry, but not before, proceed to beat the Pig violently, with the handle of a large broom. If he squeals, beat him again.

Visit the paste and beat the Pig alternately for some days, and ascertain if at the end of that period the whole is about to turn into Gosky Patties. If it does not then, it never will; and in that case the Pig may be let loose and the whole process may be considered as finished.

Conversion Table

Editors' note: Lucan and Gray use imperial measures (pounds and ounces for weight, feet and inches for length, etc) in defiance of the modern trend. This is, of course, part of their style. Despite the inconvenience, we have thought it best to respect this, and not to impose a metric system where none was intended. We recognize, however, that many readers and cooks today no longer possess imperial scales, measuring jugs, thermometers and rulers, and have therefore provided the following conversion table, which is correct to two decimal places at sea level. (For those cooking in extreme barometric conditions - e.g. in mountain refuges, unpressurised aircraft, submarines, etc - we recommend a correction factor of +/- 0.05% per kilogram of atmospheric pressure at origin. This is in accordance with the 1955 Loughborough Convention. No further adjustment is necessary for climate or latitude.)

1 ounce (oz) = 28.35 grammes	1 inch = 2.54 centimeters
1 pound (lb) = 453.6 grammes	1 foot = 30.48 centimeters
1 pint = 0.568 litre	

Oven temperatures:

Gas mark	Fahrenheit	Celsius
1	275	140
2	300	150
3	325	160
4	350	180
5	375	190
6	400	200
7	425	220
8	450	230
9	475	240

To convert degrees Fahrenheit to degrees Celsius: $C = \frac{5}{9}(F - 32)$